The Business of Excellence

The Business of Excellence

Building high-performance teams and organizations

Justin Hughes

Bloomsbury Business

An imprint of Bloomsbury Publishing Plc

BLOOMSBURY

LONDON · OXFORD · NEW YORK · NEW DELHI · SYDNEY

Bloomsbury Business
An imprint of Bloomsbury Publishing Plc

50 Bedford Square	1385 Broadway
London	New York
WC1B 3DP	NY 10018
UK	USA

www.bloomsbury.com

BLOOMSBURY and the Diana logo are trademarks of Bloomsbury Publishing Plc

First published 2016

British Library Cataloguing-in-Publication Data
A catalogue record for this book is available from the British Library.

ISBN:HB: 978-1-4729-3022-4
ePDF: 978-1-4729-3024-8
ePub: 978-1-4729-3023-1

Cover design by Sharon Mah
Cover image © RAF Red Arrows © Stephen Foote / Alamy Stock Photo
Author Photo © Max Farrant

Library of Congress Cataloging-in-Publication Data
A catalog record for this book is available from the Library of Congress.

Typeset by Newgen Knowledge Works (P) Ltd., Chennai, India
Printed and bound in India

To Alexandra and Charlotte

Anything is possible

Contents

List of figures

Acknowledgements

While one person tends to take the credit (or blame!) for a book, moving from idea to finished product has benefitted from support, inputs and effort from too many people to mention, but I do want to try to do justice to those to whom I owe most.

My wife Ann has been unequivocally supportive despite my poor deadline management meaning that my workload was heaviest in the run-up to Christmas, which coincided with her being eight months pregnant. Thank you also to my mother for her help in that period and for too many other things to mention. And it's fair to say that the project might never have come to fruition at all without the support of Ian Hallsworth and Bloomsbury; I consider it a great privilege to have the support of such a reputable publisher.

Writing a book is not something I have rushed into and the seeds were first planted by Kevin Wooff around 2006. That mantle was taken up more recently by my business partner, Jas Hawker. Many have influenced my thinking, and those directly relevant to this book have been acknowledged in the text or the notes. Of my personal contacts, Hugh Griffiths was an early catalyst and thought leader for me when I founded my business; Dr Simon Brown was my first guide on the subject of behavioural safety; and more recently Drs Stephen Bungay and John Thorogood have been more than generous with their time and expertise, as was Lord Rose of Monewden with his personal insights into life as the CEO of Marks & Spencer.

Dave Gourlay and Kelvin Truss almost certainly signed up for more than they imagined as proof readers, whilst Amy Cruickshank found that her job specification changed somewhat when she turned out to have excellent reviewing and researching skills. I am indebted to all. Thank you also to Ferranti Design for the illustrations.

Finally, I would like to thank all those others who have been part of the Mission Excellence journey; without you, none of this would have been possible:

Jez Attridge, Benny Ball, Tom Barrett, Simon Batt, Melissa Braumann, Andy Brown, Chris Carder, Duncan Clark, Keith Considine, Alison Darling, Olivia Carlish, Damian Ellacott, Myles Garland, John Green, Gemma Hardy, Andy Holland, Rog Holmes, Karin Janssen, Spike Jepson, Russ Jones, Andrew Keith, Brian Kemp, Dorota Kleina, Suzanna Lawrence, Mike Ling, Susana Lorena, Chris Lyndon-Smith, Kerry Maloney, Ian McCombie, Mark McNulty, Nicky Moore, Ed Moran, John Peters, Ben Plank, Phil Roberts, Ian Smith, Clive Soffe, Garry Stratford, Elaine Taylor, Nicky Thomas, Matt Thornton, Al Thorogood, Marek Turowski, Rick Offord, Adrian Tait, Matt Vardy, John Warner, John Watson, Rich Wells, David Withington, Andy Wyatt and Mark Zanker.

Introduction

Chapter 1

The crux of the issue

No plan survives first contact with the enemy.

Helmuth von Moltke
Chief of Staff, Prussian Army, 1857–87

Fly the plane

It was August 2001. I was a formation aerobatic pilot on the Red Arrows, the UK Royal Air Force's aerobatic display team comprising nine pilots flying Hawk jet training aircraft. We were due to display at Eastbourne on the south coast of England. It was a typical English summer's day: raining, hazy, and with low cloud over the sea. We started the show and, as we completed the first manoeuvre, the leader turned the formation out to sea. However, the haze had quickly rolled in much thicker and suddenly we were in cloud. And not just any old cloud, but really thick cloud. We had been flying approximately 5m away from each other and all of a sudden, I couldn't see the aircraft next to me.

As the pilots started to lose sight of the aircraft around them, one by one they started to break out of the formation and we ended up in cloud, in five sections of aircraft, underneath airspace used by London's Gatwick Airport for commercial traffic. One minute I was flying the display, in a zone of what the psychologists would call 'unconscious competence',[1] the next minute I was on my own, in cloud, travelling at a speed of around 400mph (640kph) at 1000ft (300m) at some funny angle relative to the sea, with eight other jets, which I couldn't see, not far away in the cloud. How do you resolve a situation like that, which jumps from business as usual to impending disaster within the blink of an eye? Where do you even start?

In order to answer that question, I need to offer you some further insight into being a military fighter pilot. If you asked somebody what are the core skills or competencies required in flying, they may offer suggestions such as having good spatial awareness, keen hand-eye coordination, excellent eyesight and so on. I wouldn't argue with any of these things … when you are learning to fly. However, by the time you are operating high-performance jets, these are simply the prerequisites.

When you first start to learn, it takes all of your mental capacity just to fly the plane in a straight line and respond to the radio. Over time though, the basics become embedded in your subconscious. Muscle memory and pattern recognition do a lot of the job for you, and you become much more effective at prioritizing your time and focus, and so have excess brainpower freed up for other more advanced tasks. And you need this spare capacity to *operate* the aircraft. A modern high-performance jet has more information coming in, and more things going on at once, than the pilot could possibly digest in the time available. So operating a jet is, as much as anything else, an exercise in mul-titasking and prioritizing. The ability to do this well is the difference between an exceptional and average fighter pilot.

You see this same pattern in the acquisition of almost any new skill. At first, you are fumbling and having to concentrate on every single aspect. Over time, patterns and actions become memorized and automatic and you start to focus on the subtleties or advanced skills that were ini-tially completely beyond you. The corollary to this is that often what is happening in front of you (the pattern) has too many variables to take them all in, but once you have seen the pattern enough times, you start to recognize variations from the pattern even without isolating all the variables.[2]

This concept also holds true even when building on skills starting from an advanced level. When I started training on the Red Arrows, I was already an experienced fighter pilot, but more than once I would watch the video of the practice display and realize that I had not turned the smoke on for a particular manoeuvre. And yet on the radio, which was overlaid onto the video, you could clearly hear the leader calling 'smoke on go'. How could one not hear that? It was absolutely loud and clear. The issue was that I was concentrating on the basics (staying in the right position – nothing was subconscious at that stage) to such a degree that I had no spare mental capacity to even notice what was being said on the radio.

The ability to multitask and prioritize assumes that you know exactly what the priorities are at any moment in time, something which is difficult to achieve in a dynamic environment. In practice, the more complex the world you are operating in, the simpler the priorities need to be to fall back on.[3] And you need to have worked them out in advance; you won't come up with brilliant priorities in the heat of the moment, facing a high-stress situation for which you have done no relevant preparation. In the example I described, there is simply too much going on too fast to try and produce a watertight plan of action. And there is certainly no time for a committee meeting. Fortunately in aviation we have some very simple clear priorities:

Aviate – Navigate – Communicate.

There is no point being lost (navigating), trying to work out your position and talking to somebody about the problem on the radio (communicating) if you're crashing into the sea at the time. What's the ball you can't afford to drop? Aviate. Fly the plane.

Back at Eastbourne in the cloud, I focused my attention on the flight instruments and rolled the aircraft the right way up. I started climbing away from the sea and turned away from the last-known position of the rest of the formation. I then checked my map for the height of the Gatwick airspace. By doing those things, and only those things (the most important things) first, I could now actually pause and assess. Nothing else needed doing immediately.

What do you think that the team leader did in this situation? Bear in mind that the leader has professional, moral and legal responsibility for the safety of the crowd and the pilots. Plus, this is the military after all; there is a clearly defined line of accountability. It had just gone about as badly wrong as it could do. There is a realistic chance of a crash, either a mid-air collision or someone flying into the sea. Imagine the pressure that individual is under in that moment, not quite knowing where everybody is or what is happening. The temptation to jump in and attempt to exert control would be almost overwhelming.

Initially, he just flew his own plane. There would be no point trying to micromanage the team while he was crashing himself. And while he was doing that, he gave everybody a few seconds (time is quite compressed here) to sort out their own lives. He resisted the temptation to try and over-control. When you use words like trust and empowerment, situations like this are when they really count. There was nothing he could do for those first few seconds and he recognized that, trusting people to do whatever was needed to be done to look after themselves in a way that would not exacerbate the situation.

After a short interval, he did come on the radio and check everybody's height and position, organized the formation and deconflicted before heading to a meeting point. That was the end of the show that day, but a potentially catastrophic situation had been quickly and effectively resolved through self-discipline on the part of the individual pilots (no one jumping in or panicking), each flying his own aircraft to minimize the risk to anyone else, and clear thinking under pressure. None of these things happened by accident.

You may think that was all very interesting but has absolutely no relevance whatsoever to you, your team or your job. And you may not sit strapped to your chair breathing oxygen through a tube like a pilot does, but just think about this situation in a slightly different context. Imagine doing your job, working very hard but being on top of it. Then you are distracted by a major issue requiring all of your attention; meanwhile the rest of the team are still highly reliant on you not to let them down, and you also need to keep on top of the other hundred things all simultaneously competing for your attention.

The preceding story is not really about flying planes. It's about execution. And not just any execution; it's about *mission* execution rather than *task* execution. The point is that we are measured on achieving an outcome, irrespective of what changes along the way. Compliance with a plan may be a powerful enabler, but is not the measure of success. And the outcome has to be achieved in a highly demanding environment.

Like many people in large organizations, a fighter pilot has to deliver results in a world characterized by ambiguity, an overload of imperfect information and conflicting priorities. It's also an environment where failure is not an option and mistakes cost lives. There is a requirement to deal with all of the above issues and still get it right first time. In business terms, it's about delivering outcomes quarter on quarter, every quarter, and consistently exceeding expectations. In sport, it's about winning week in, week out. In NGOs, it's about aligning multiple stake-holders to meet others' needs quickly and effectively. The measures of success may be different; however, the challenges – and, as we will see, many of the principles of the solution – are the same.

World-class basics

In 2009, I was the guest speaker at a dinner for sports coach UK. Attending the meeting were coaches and support staff working with elite sportsmen and women across the whole sporting spectrum, including a number of international delegates. You might ask what a retired, 'slightly' out of shape fighter pilot (specialist sport: armchair rugby critic) could possibly tell this audience about the pursuit of sporting excellence, something which crossed my own mind more than once. However, not for the first time as a speaker, I fell back on the advice given to me about presenting by Sir George Cox. When he was director general of the Institute of Directors, Cox was given the rather daunting task of briefing the chancellor, the chairman of the Bank of England and the chairman of the Federal Reserve on an economic issue. Having fretted for some time about what he could possibly tell such an august audience, he eventually concluded, 'If they're not interested in my opinion, they shouldn't have bloody well asked me!'

At the dinner, I was seated next to (now Sir) Ian McGeechan, an icon in the coaching world, in particular in sports coaching. For once the term 'icon' is probably appropriate here. Two months later, McGeechan took the British and Irish Lions, a scratch international rugby squad who had never played together before, and came within one penalty of defeating South Africa, the reigning world champions, in a Test series played at home for the South Africans. It was not strictly a coincidence that I was seated next to Ian, having covertly manipulated the seating plan, and I made the most of the opportunity to have him as a captive audience, completely monopolizing him for most of the evening.

After my presentation, I asked him what it is that makes the difference in teams that win consistently over time. It seemed to me that in soccer, excessive financial rewards, fame and ego can have a significant negative impact on the team dynamic. In contrast, in professional rugby not even the big stars received really crazy money (in the UK premiership, there was a salary cap in place); there were no billionaire owners or clubs raking in millions, so no team could effectively buy success; teams had access to broadly similar resources and technology; and there was a fairly liquid transfer market. And yet some teams, whether national or international, seemed to win again and again over the long term. Ian had coached some of these teams. What was the secret? Ian paused and leaned over to me: 'Look mate, it's not rocket science, we're only kicking a funny-shaped ball around playing rugby; you need to understand what factors will make the difference in winning or losing a game. Those factors are often pretty simple basic aspects of the game, but you need to be better than anybody else in the world at *those* things. It's all about world-class basics. . . '.

Learning from experience

The above observations are an important anchor point for everything that follows and align with my own experience on two levels. In my first career as an RAF fighter pilot, I had extensive first-hand experience of the benefits of getting the basics right, and also the intrinsic reward and sense of purpose that come with the pursuit of excellence. And like every customer, I have experienced too many times a level of service in which the basics could not have been further from world class.

As much as anything, this is a book about world-class basics. I aim to cut through the noise to focus on what really matters. My approach is empirical rather than theoretical, from experience, observation and deep thought to explanation; however, I believe that the line of logic is no less intellectually rigorous for that. It seems to me that there is a group of academics, consultants and trainers who use theory to complicate and to offer an illusion of precision, in particular around planning, decision-making and managing risk, areas where such an illusion can be a dangerous one. Faced with ambiguity, imperfect data and under time pressure, I would rather be approximately right than precisely wrong.

Many others have contributed to my thinking, and the most significant are acknowledged at the start of this book. However, the primary sources of material were the twelve years spent as an RAF fighter pilot and a further thirteen years spent building Mission Excellence, a consultancy specializing in team and organizational performance. I have drawn heavily on my military experience, although my working career actually started at a fairly senior position in the food retail industry … I quickly achieved the dizzy heights of 'two stars', cooking burgers and cleaning floors at McDonalds!

After a year in the army, I studied physics at university, with slightly less diligence than I might have done in hindsight, and after a year of travel through Southeast Asia and Australia, I joined the RAF and spent the next twelve years flying jets. After the first three years of training, I spent six years on the front line flying the Tornado F3, taking part in training and operational deployments all over the world. I amassed around 1,500 flight hours on the Tornado and was then lucky enough to be selected for the Red Arrows. Between 1965 and the end of 2015, the team had done over 4,700 displays in 56 countries. I flew for three years as a display pilot between 2000 and 2002, including around 250 displays worldwide, becoming the executive officer and deputy team leader. I eventually left the RAF at the end of my time with the Red Arrows, with over 3,000 hours' total flying time.

At that point, at the end of 2002, I founded Mission Excellence. To this day, client-facing personnel are predominantly from operational backgrounds, including several other ex-fighter pilots; they bring a first-hand experience and knowledge of what it takes to deliver results in high pressure, complex and fast-moving environments. They know what works and what doesn't. We have worked with over 100 clients around the world, ranging from instantly recognizable global corporations to professional sport, and not-for-profit public sector bodies and charities, in addition to contributing to risk management and execution-related programmes at the University of Oxford and several top business schools.

While Mission Excellence draws on the latest thinking and experience from a wide variety of sources, both in this book and on client engagements, we often use the military as a case study, not because the military always provides the benchmark in excellence or any panacea solutions, but because militaries have been grappling with the challenge of execution in large, complex organizations, often operating globally, for many hundreds of years. In 1792, the British Navy had 100,000 crew operating 661 vessels around the world, engaged in both military and peace-keeping activities, without any of the communication tools which we now take for granted. The execution may not always have been perfect, but much of the learning has already been done.

If that is true and the answers are in the public domain, then what is so difficult about execution and delivering excellence? We know how to do it. Unfortunately, knowing is not the same as doing. And herein lies the difference between average and excellent. Closing the 'execution gap' – the gap between what gets talked about and planned, and what is actually delivered – requires one to develop independent thought, objectivity, organizational skills and the ability to engage people. Simple concepts such as stripping situations back to the facts, accepting personal accountability and being prepared to hold others to account are actually not that common in practice. And the picture becomes even more confused when one adds in the effect of the 'real world' on the execution of plans, not to mention the subtleties of ego, personal agenda, hierarchy and flawed reward schemes.

Over the last thirteen years as an entrepreneur and consultant, I have had the opportunity to dissect and better understand the relevance of my experience as a fighter pilot to many other environments. The military tends to be very good at implementation and some aspects of leadership, while fighter pilots, whether they realize it or not, tend to be additionally very able in areas like dealing with ambiguous situations, agility and decision-making under pressure. The reasons are invariably based on hard won experience, which means that processes and behaviours have evolved rather than been designed. This evolution means that the solutions are very robust – they work – but that it's not always easy to capture them. One has to reverse-engineer the theory or the model.

I have also had the opportunity to learn *from* other environments. My consulting and development clients have ranged from global brand names to family-owned businesses and from world championship-winning sports franchises to the founders of a social enterprise. In addition to that work, I have also walked the talk and been a partner in two other start-ups in medical conferences and in retail. I have stepped out of the former now and it has successfully grown for almost ten years, while the latter, started just before the 2008 financial crash, provided a rather more brutal learning curve, from which I emerged relatively unscathed, albeit a little poorer and a lot wiser.

In this book, I have presented a model for high performance that has been twenty-five years in its evolution and tested in the most demanding of operating environments. If the concepts appear simple, that is the aim, but it took a long time to get to this point. With a clear understanding of what we are trying to achieve and what we are up against, together with a proven easily understood approach to cut through the noise and stack the odds of decisive success in our favour, anything is possible.

The crux of the issue

My starting point is my first career and the relevance of that to business. What do fighter pilots actually do? Well, if you've seen the movie *Top Gun*, you'll have an opinion; unfortunately, however, it's not much like that. And if that's disappointing for you, trust me, it was a whole lot more disappointing for me. I saw that movie when I was a student, thought that flying jets looked like the coolest job ever and I signed up for twelve years. Sadly, there was no Californian beach volleyball, no taking photos of the bad guys while chewing gum and flying in formation upside down 12 inches from their cockpit, and no Hollywood superstars. The sort of flying you see in *Top Gun* actually does happen to some extent, once you remove the Hollywood add-ons; however, the flying is only the core functional skill, the basic tool of the job. You have to get to the stage as a fighter pilot where you can perform that core skill using only 10 per cent of your mental capacity. The other 90 per cent is used to *operate* the aircraft, to do something with it as part of a much wider multidisciplinary, cross-functional mission team, and to deliver outcomes.

The problem

I have already highlighted some of the challenges of the fighter pilot's environment: ambiguity, information overload, time pressure and the high consequences of failure. He or she works within, and as part of, a clearly defined line management structure but actually does the day job as part of a matrix cross-functional team, often working with other individuals and teams over whom they have no line authority, and who may be in fact be sharing their time with other users of their services. This environment requires agility, since the one thing you can guarantee on a fighter mission is that 'no plan survives first contact with the enemy' or, in business terms perhaps, 'no plan survives first contact with the real world', whether that be the customer, competitor or economic environment.

Execution must be carried out in a world where it is only possible to control a small number of the variables. Ultimately, the only relevant measure of success is our ability to deliver outcomes or effects; we execute the mission, not the plan. If we can consistently close the gap between the desired and actual outcomes with a myriad of obstacles to be overcome, and other people actually trying to cause us to fail, then surely this is excellence.

The same challenge faced by fighter pilots was particularly well articulated by experienced management consultant, academic and military historian Stephen Bungay in his book *The Art of Action*.[4] Bungay described an iterative process illustrated in Figure 1.1.

We start with a desired outcome, and so we make plans. Because of those plans, people take actions, which then deliver actual outcomes.

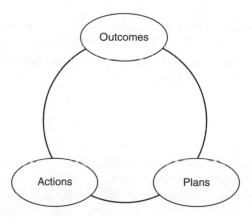

Figure 1.1 Outcomes, plans and actions

Unfortunately, with no further refinement, on a large-scale task subject to the influence of external factors, the chance of the desired and actual outcomes coinciding is slim to nil.

First, plans are always made with imperfect information. There are things you don't know, and things you can't know. And even if the plan was perfect, why don't people ever do what you told them to? Even if the plan was perfect and people did exactly what you told them to, you probably still wouldn't achieve what you intended due to changes in the external environment, the plan not surviving first contact with the real world, reallocation of resources or any of the other factors outside your control.

Bungay openly admits that he is not the first to grapple with this issue. The crux of the problem just described can be summed up in one word: friction. It was first used in this context by Carl von Clausewitz (1780–1831), a famous strategist in the Prussian Army, to describe the combination of confusion, random events and network effects that make large-scale military conflict inherently unpredictable and impossible to centrally control, as opposed to direct, an alternative which is both more practical and in fact, the only rational solution. The essence of the difference is that a controller wants people to do only what they are told, while a director offers clear guidance and support, but empowers and trusts others to work out their own solutions. In just the same way as a ball rolled across soft sand will quickly slow down due to the effect of friction, Clausewitz used a similar analogy to describe the effect of the real world on the attempted execution of plans.

The solution

So what's the solution? Better data gathering? More and more detailed plans? More communication so that people have no excuse for not knowing *exactly* what is expected of them? Extra controls in place to make sure that people do what they are supposed to? Not quite ...

Clausewitz's ideas were developed and practically applied by Helmuth von Moltke the Elder (1800–1891) who was Chief of Staff of the Prussian Army for thirty years. He worked out that, in simple terms, the solution was a combination of absolute clarity in strategic direction and goals, together with flexibility in execution. While von Moltke was certainly not the first military leader to successfully employ empowerment and decentralized execution, he may well have been the first to combine intellectual rigour with practical application on a large scale, and certainly the first to have his history and methods captured in such detail. It is worth noting that the Prussians are widely accepted to be the most skilled and successful army of the latter half of the nineteenth century and the early twentieth century. The execution principles honed by von Moltke still hold true and are reflected in military strategy to this day, not to mention a few corporate approaches; Jack Welch, former CEO of General Electric, was a student of von Moltke.

As a keen student of military history, Bungay realized that the challenges he observed in twenty-first-century businesses were no different to those faced by Clausewitz and von Moltke, and that the solution was also no different. Not more plans, but fewer plans. Instead of making enormously complex detailed tactical plans for a whole year, during which time everything will change, only make plans for a realistically short time horizon and then re-evaluate. Instead of more communication, less but better communication is required. And instead of more controls, better clarity about desired outcomes (the 'what' and 'why'), but more flexibility in how they are achieved. Focus on the outcome;

don't make achieving the measures or execution of the plan into the goal in itself. Don't turn the means into the end. That is not to write off the importance of planning – a whole section of this book is devoted to it. However it is the planning, rather than the plan, which adds the value.

Clausewitz, von Moltke and Bungay were all grappling with strategic-level organizational issues. However, friction is surely present at the individual mission level too. When operating fighter jets, the speed of change, the requirement for agility in response to the external operating environment and the number of both independent and interdependent variables at play, mean that von Moltke's thinking is just as applicable. Plans are detailed only for short-term targets, until the impact of those activities in progressing towards operational and strategic outcomes can be measured. The aim is not lost in the noise of some long-term plan designed to win a personal bonus or tick some key performance indicator boxes, but defined in such a way that the mission, the reason for it and why it is important, are crystal clear. Communication is concise and clear. There is real clarity in task, roles and the allocation of resources. Execution itself is conducted with defined simple priorities and objectives, decentralized decision-making authority, and freedom to manoeuvre within agreed boundaries or parameters.

The military sum up the competencies required by officers, or within the organization more generally, as command, management and leadership. The relative weighting changes with role and responsibility, but all three need to be present to some extent. Bungay replaces command with direction, while we prefer direction, leadership and execution, and, in contrast to both of the sources mentioned, I present them as a hierarchy as in Figure 1.2.

1. Direction is the ability to set and articulate clear direction, to provide vision, or more accurately 'intent'. This might be referred to as doing the right thing. This is predominantly an intellectual activity predicated on critical and creative thinking, and communication skills, and becomes more relevant in more senior roles.
2. Leadership is the ability to bring others with you on the journey, such that they *choose* to follow of their own free will (otherwise it becomes an issue of seniority, not leadership). This is predominantly a moral

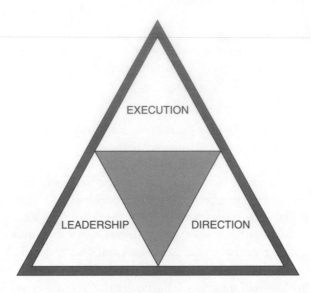

Figure 1.2 The hierarchy of organizational performance

and emotional activity based on one's values and behaviours and is valid at all levels within an organization.

3. Execution is the ability to deliver results and get things done – what might be referred to as doing things right. This is a physical activity – something happens as a result; it is a function of people, clarity in task and roles, planning, management of time and resources, and learning for continual improvement.

The model is presented like it is, as a triangle, in order to reflect a structure or hierarchy between the competencies and the fact that Direction and Leadership are key enablers of Execution. Execution is the thing which gets measured – the delivery of results, which is itself a function of both behavioural and process issues. Direction is a prerequisite, to provide clarity in priorities and intent; it is essentially a 'push' factor, pointing people in the right direction or applying the Execution to the right problem. Leadership, on the other hand, is a 'pull' factor, bringing others with you; it is, in some ways, the icing on the cake. With clear direction and strong operational performance, you can actually survive without great leadership (and many do), however it is the thing which can make the single biggest difference in improving performance.

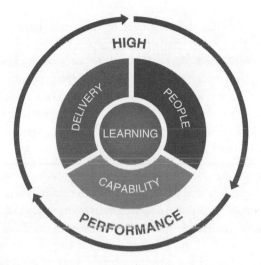

Figure 1.3 High-performance model

The crux of the issue in team and organizational performance is never one simple factor but the ability to close the gap that inevitably opens up at the point of the inconvenient collision of desire, motivation, plans and actions with the real world. Closing this gap requires a certain type of behaviour from individuals, alignment of thought and effort but decentralization in execution, a disciplined outcome-focused approach to delivery and a deeply embedded culture of learning.

I have combined these factors into a sequential model for high performance, shown in its simplified format in Figure 1.3. This model is the result of 25 years' professional experience, learning, reflection and refinement, and forms the basis for the remainder of this book from Chapter 3 onwards.

- **People** – selecting and developing people; the primacy of behaviour over skills in high-performance teams
- **Capability** – building the potential to succeed and breaking down silos through common purpose, alignment and empowerment
- **Delivery** – a rigorous outcome-focused approach to execution
- **Learning** – how to learn in real time and maximize the rate of application of learning, compared to others

It should be noted that the elements of this model are primarily skills or behaviours, more than they are processes. They have to be acquired, practiced and embedded. You can no more become an expert in debriefing by learning the process than you can become an expert guitar player by learning the theory, as I am currently finding out the hard way. One only has to look at the self-help section in bookshops to see that many people are looking for the instant fix. One doesn't see any books called 'The 10-minute Heart Surgeon', so why 'The 10-minute Manager'?

The model also describes a system. In common with many systems, optimization of individual elements is not necessarily the same as optimization of the system. For instance, debriefing is a skill which can be acquired to facilitate learning – a combination of intellect, analysis and facilitation – see later. However, it is difficult to practice in isolation. If there was no clearly defined aim, no plan, a weak team dynamic and no measurement of any outcome, it will be challenging to analyse performance against the aim and against the plan, and to identify any specific learning outcomes to take forward.

Skills can never be truly mastered and the system will never be perfect. However, no matter what our start point, if we can accelerate our learning curve through continuous improvement; then it is possible for any team or organization to make high performance a reality. Execution is a goal. Excellence is a journey.

Chapter 2

Excellence – it starts with you

Excellence is not a single event, but a habit.

Aristotle

Looking in the mirror

There's no one definition of excellence; it's one of those things that we struggle to describe but we know when we see it. It's something about raising the bar beyond normal expectations, achieving a standard way beyond the average, not just doing something well, but doing it as well as it can be done. But it's not a zero sum or mutually exclusive game, where excellence is a finite resource. The top two players in the world can both be excellent in a tennis match simultaneously. It's theoretically possible for every airline to be delivering excellent service at the same time, however unlikely that scenario might seem.

It probably doesn't really matter that we don't have a single precise definition of excellence. If we intuitively know what we're talking about, and recognize it when we see it, there's little benefit in arguing about which words best describe it. However, one thing's for sure; it starts with you. This book is primarily about teams and organizations, but it's important to realize that you don't achieve excellence or high performance merely by association. It starts with the values, behaviours, attitudes and professional standards that you personally bring to the party, and that is the subject of this chapter.

Let me give you an example. Have you ever been to a badly run meeting? Not in your current role where you run the meetings, of course! Maybe in your last job, where they didn't set such high standards? Imagine arriving at a meeting that is clearly not ready to start. The chairperson is running around still sorting things out, people are continuing to arrive after the start time, the audiovisual equipment has not been checked or there has not been any rehearsal and nobody can get it to work. And during the meeting, phones keep buzzing, somebody is sending emails and people wander in and out. Not surprisingly, the meeting overruns, no real decisions of significance are made, and nobody's sure if the meeting achieved its aim, because there was no agenda. What mental programme is loaded in your head for doing business with this person again? What are their acceptable professional standards? What does this meeting say about how they do business?

Now imagine going to another meeting. A request for agenda items is circulated well in advance. The final agenda is circulated the day before. You arrive and everything is ready to go. The meeting starts on time (exactly). It is well facilitated with sufficient discussion of each item, but the chairperson does not permit too much wandering off track, and drives every item to an outcome. It finishes on time. What mental programme is loaded in your head for doing business with this person again? What are their acceptable professional standards? What does this meeting say about how they do business?

Compare the first example with something from my own experience. Soon after I started on the Red Arrows, I attended a meeting. It wasn't a sortie (flying) brief, just a routine meeting chaired by the Team Leader. The meeting was due to start at 10 a.m., so I arrived about 2 minutes early. Everybody else was already there. As the new boy, I sidled in at the back and kept quiet. But the meeting didn't start, which was a bit odd since everybody was now there. The Team Leader was just chatting away to the Manager about something, and every now and again, he would glance away from her, and down at his watch. Finally, at precisely the planned start time, he looked again at his watch and said '3, 2, 1, hack. 10 o'clock. Good morning everybody.' And the meeting started. Now I observed this behaviour, and my initial reaction was along the lines of 'This guy needs to get out a bit more; he needs to get a life.' However, over time you start to appreciate that this is the way we do business; that standard of excellence, that professionalism and that attention to detail start to permeate through everything you do. How you do the little things is how you do everything. You don't choose a different behaviour just because it's a big important job and you're under a lot of stress. In fact, it's quite the opposite; when you're really under a lot of pressure, you revert to default wired-in behaviours because you have too many other things to worry about than 'raising the bar'. The lesson about professional standards is fairly self-explanatory: excellence starts with the person you see in the mirror.

There is an amusing flip side to this focus on exact timing, which probably says more about the British psyche, and in particular the competitive psyche of a certain type of British male, than anything else (the cross section of the Red Arrows pilots has been rather male-dominated to date). The Red Arrows seem to take a perverse pride in a rather understated self-deprecating approach to excellence. Individually and collectively there is an unremitting focus on raising the bar and the pursuit of excellence. However, it's 'not very British' to be too obvious about those things. So, what happens in practice for a briefing is that everyone has their watch set correctly to the second. You know what time the briefing starts, and it is unacceptable to be late, but equally you don't want to be sitting there like a complete nerd 10 minutes beforehand. And when you sit down with 2 seconds to go, everybody else pretends they didn't even notice the perfect timing – no comment is made, because that wouldn't be cool either . . .

Setting the standard

Setting a high standard means not hiding behind excuses. To return, briefly I promise, to the theme of punctuality (it's such a nice simple example), I have heard just about every excuse in response to my point about starting meetings on time. They vary from the generic ('What can you do, some people will always be late') to the specific ('But the customer is at the heart of everything we do, and I might need to take a call from a huge client which allows us to close off the deal of the year'). The latter is easily put to bed. The one time that call comes through, no problem – you can be late for my meeting. But don't tell me that's the reason every other time when you simply weren't organized.

The concept of people always being late is a more interesting one, in particular when people hide behind the excuses of organizational culture or national traits. By way of example, southern Europe appears to adopt a rather different cultural norm to northern Europe on this issue. Now I'm not recommending for a second that you should embark on a crusade to change the time-keeping culture of half of Europe, but you can definitely change it on a local level. People are generally late, either because the leader is himself often late (we will look at the symbolism of a leader's behaviour and the 'shadow of the leader' in the chapter on leadership) or because they know that it is an accepted norm and there will be no accountability for lateness.

This is a remarkably easy norm to change at a local level. Some years ago I attended a really excellent negotiating skills course. The joining instructions were rather curt and to the point, stating that delegates should meet in the reception centre bar at 17.50. Something in my personality or military background immediately alerted me to the fact that this was an unusual start time, and was probably intended to demonstrate a point of some sort. Sure enough, when we grouped, the facilitator arrived exactly on time. One person was a minute or two late; having ascertained this, the facilitator simply looked at his watch, raised an eyebrow and waited in silence for their arrival. Then another person needed to return to their room to pick up their reading glasses. Again the facilitator waited in silence. When we were finally all assembled, the facilitator asked, 'Are we now ready?' and proceeded to lead us to the classroom. For the session that evening, the facilitator was polite and professional at all times, but never used more words than he needed to and made no attempt to initiate any social interaction. He laid down the ground rules on phones, punctuality and toilet breaks in a way which didn't invite feedback or transgression.

In the classroom, there were water bottles and glasses on a side ledge, but he never invited anyone to help themselves and no one asked for water. Over dinner, I ended up sitting next to the facilitator and tried to initiate a conversation. He answered my questions with a minimum of detail, and no more; he never asked me anything. After a short while, I got bored and ate the rest of my meal in silence.

During the next morning, a point arose in the classroom, where I spontaneously offered a short anecdote from my own experience to reinforce the lesson. The facilitator politely let me finish, made no comment or thank you, and continued as if my contribution had never happened; nobody else made any spontaneous contributions.

The facilitator continued this behaviour until lunchtime of the second day, when he suddenly relaxed and asked much more warmly what people thought of the course and his behaviour so far? It emerged that he had been playing a game: a simple example of how easy it is to dominate an interaction and manipulate people's behaviours using some basic psychology. During that opening 18 hours, no one had been late once, no one had asked for a toilet break, there had been no interruptions from mobile phones, and no one asked for a drink of water. He did establish at this point that people had noticed the water and would have liked a drink. He asked people how normal this disciplined behaviour was and found that it was almost unheard of for this group.

One might argue that the point could have been made in rather less than 18 hours, but it was well made nonetheless, in this case about maintaining psychological advantage and the balance of power in a negotiation. However, even with a more positive application, the lesson is the same. If you're the team leader, the chairperson or the boss, what you project will get reflected back at you. Once you start to gain a reputation for starting meetings on time, for 'running a tight ship', for being firm but fair, people start to behave accordingly. It's all about the standard that you personally set. And remember, how you do the little things is how you do the big things . . .

The humility of high performers

While setting dizzily high standards and consistently holding themselves to them, many high performers possess another trait that might be more surprising: humility. While some who are near the top of their game appear at times to have a self-belief that might border on arrogance, for those right at the very top, no matter what they project, that rarely actually becomes arrogance. In fact, they often never really believe that they are actually quite as good as everybody else says. They are almost paranoid about failing to achieve, about not being able to pull off the same results again. They recognize the twin dangers of complacency and arrogance, and behind the determination and self-belief, there is some sort of inner paranoia that constantly drives them on to greater heights. Certainly, in some of the most inspirational leaders of teams and organizations, it is more common to see humility. They really don't believe their own press, and genuinely think that they might only be where they are due to luck, timing and being surrounded by good people.

This humility can evidence itself in many different ways. Consider legendary US investor Warren Buffet, for some time the world's richest man, and someone who is certainly under no illusion as to the uniqueness of his talents. Buffet possibly has a better track record than anybody else in his lifetime, and probably for a much longer period, as an investor delivering growth consistently over the long term. Many would consider his clarity of thought to be bordering on genius. However, Buffet himself is a strong subscriber to his own 'Ovarian Lottery' theory, that no matter what intellect he might have, if it wasn't for the fact that he was born in the time and place that he was (United States, good education, relatively under-analysed stock markets in his early years), his success would never have happened.

The role of factors other than natural talent in success has been explored, among others, by Malcolm Gladwell in *Outliers*[1] and Matthew Syed in *Bounce*.[2] Both examined the balance of talent versus hard work in high performers in very different fields, and both come down fairly strongly on the primacy of effort over ability. Gladwell even goes so far as to reverse engineer a theory that 10,000 hours is the magic number of hours of immersion or practice common to many high performers. While the 10,000 hour argument is some way from being scientifically rigorous (it's a nice soundbite!), it is common sense to me that intense focus and investing much more effort than everybody else stacks the odds of achieving mastery and success in your favour; it may actually fall into statements of the blindingly obvious. Gladwell also explores another line of thinking to explain logically why some people have natural advantage due to some combination of timing and circumstance – for example, the oldest children in a school year tend to have advantages due to size and maturity in competitive sport – which then becomes self-reinforcing. This would be akin to Buffet's 'Ovarian Lottery'.

So, despite whatever natural talent may or may not exist, luck and timing will often be significant factors in success, as they may have been for Buffet and almost certainly are for the oldest children in the class. But those factors are largely outside of our control. And not many will argue with the 10,000 hour concept, even if the precision of the specific number is open to debate. However, even when life's dice reveal a good throw, and after you factor in for some hard work, there is still something about the mindset of many high performers that raises them above the crowd.

Some years ago, I was speaking at a conference and was fortunate enough to have lunch with Sebastian (Lord) Coe, Olympic gold medal winner, former world-record holder and more recently chairman of the London 2012 Olympic Bid and then Organizing Committee. I talked to Coe about debriefing and the role of truly objective self-review of performance on the Red Arrows, and how rare that seemed to be in the commercial world. He too didn't understand the low importance often placed on that sort of review mechanism. He described how even when he was winning gold medals and breaking records all over the world, he would listen to anybody who had an interesting opinion on improving his performance – he was always looking for a new insight or something else to 'gain the edge'.

There was an amusing follow-on to this story more recently in a newspaper interview he and Steve Ovett gave jointly. Ovett was another British world-class middle distance runner in the 1980s; Coe and Ovett regularly shared the honours, but it was common knowledge that there was no love lost between them. The interview occurred many years later and was one of the few occasions when they had been together since their glory years. Coe described Christmas Day one year, when he had been out running and was in two minds about whether to do a second run that day – it was Christmas Day after all. Then he thought 'I bet *he* [Ovett] is running twice,' and he went out and did a second really hard training session in the evening, after the family lunch. When he told this story in the interview, Ovett paused before responding, 'You only ran twice?'

For a more recent example, it was interesting to see the actions of New Zealand All Blacks rugby captain Richie McCaw during the 2015 World Cup. Regarded by many as the greatest rugby player of all time, McCaw was rested for one game to allow a minor injury to recover. Faced with the option to sit a game out in the stands and relax, McCaw actually put his kit on the same as usual and became the team's water bottle carrier for the day, a role more often carried out by support staff.

The sort of humility demonstrated by Buffet, Coe and McCaw among others, was identified as a factor in some of the most successful business leaders by Jim Collins in his book, *Good to Great*.[3] Collins conducted empirical research on company performance and correlated it with the tenure and leadership style of the chief executive. His conclusion was that the true leadership stars were not the super high-profile personalities, who often had a good run for a short time before becoming distracted or a victim of their own success; performance was rarely if ever sustainable when everything revolved around one individual. Real long-term out-performance was unsurprisingly rare, but was most likely with a different type of leader, whom Collins calls the 'level 5 leader'.

The 'level 5' refers to Collins' hierarchy of types of leader: highly capable individual, contributing team member, competent manager, effective leader and executive. Collins identifies the key qualities of a level 5 leader as an individual who blends extreme personal humility with intense professional will. If this seems an unlikely combination, that would explain its rarity. However, when one thinks about it, the concept scores pretty well on the common sense test. An executive with clear direction, drive, focus and tenacity, but who also retains the self-awareness to know that he will not always be right, that others may have equal or greater talent, that there are other factors at play as well as his own ability, and to be open-minded about learning, is much more likely to be successful than peers not displaying those traits.

High performers often do not believe their own press. They possess a rare combination of determination, self-belief and humility; they are relentless in their pursuit of excellence.

Leave no stone unturned

Another aspect of Coe's story was his desire and ability to do something about his real or perceived weaknesses, that is, the desire and ability to learn. Not only would he objectively review his performance to see how he could improve when he was already the best in the world, he was actively looking for any new idea that might add some tiny performance increment. I should add a warning that this concept needs to be applied carefully. Coe was at the top of his game and, with all the primary factors largely addressed and under control, could afford the relative luxury of focusing on the details. The inherent assumption about the primary factors is important. Often we are resource-limited in how many issues we can address, in which case it is important to have clear priorities as to which levers to pull to get the biggest 'bang for your buck'. If you can only pull one lever, make sure you are pulling the one that delivers the most value.

I heard a nice example of this recently from a successful entrepreneur. Some years previously, he had been out partying in London's Soho district, and he and his friend ended up in a nightclub talking to the owner. The owner bemoaned the fact that he was making no money. After trying to single-handedly make some short-term impact on that issue, via his bar purchases, the entrepreneur offered to buy the nightclub. The two party guys returned the next day and had a slightly more serious conversation about terms, after which they owned a nightclub, at which point they started to take the concept more seriously. It turned out that in Soho it is all but impossible not to make money on Thursday, Friday and Saturday. And it is all but impossible to make money on Sunday, Monday and Tuesday. And so rather than worrying about all the things you could do to make the club a more attractive proposition, they first focused on how to make more money on Wednesdays. They realized that most clubs, including theirs, put the headline DJ and entertainment on at the weekend. But they were packed every weekend, no matter what the quality of entertainment (within some common sense limits), and so they moved their best DJ to Wednesday. Pretty soon the club was *the* place to go on Wednesdays. Only then did they focus on the next priority. Two years later, they sold out at a considerable profit. With limited time and resources, be sure to solve the right problem, as opposed to producing the right solution to the wrong problem.

This chapter is not about compromise, however, or being good enough. It is about the relentless pursuit of excellence. Having addressed all the big performance issues, Coe was in search of the next level. His approach of absorbing knowledge from every conceivable source is also common to Sir Clive Woodward, head coach to England's World Cup-winning rugby squad, and Sir Dave Brailsford, the cycling supremo, who transformed British Cycling into a genuinely world-beating team and built Team Sky from a zero base into winners of the Tour de France three times in four years.[4]

Woodward was undoubtedly fortunate in having an inspirational captain, Martin Johnson, to lead his team, and one could argue that he inherited a golden generation of players at the optimum time. But it is also true that he transformed this golden generation into world-beaters, and that he brought a standard of professionalism, which was previously absent, to every aspect of England's preparation and operations. He was, and is, a student of high performance, and has an obsessive attention to detail. He was prepared to consider almost any idea, no matter how outlandish, in striving for an edge. Being open-minded that somebody might know a better way of doing it is another surprisingly rare trait. Sources of influence on Woodard's thinking on rugby performance included an Australian dentist (who discovered what was really important in running a business after a nervous breakdown),[5] an external management consultant, a vision specialist (in the ocular sense) and the Royal Marines. No stone was left unturned.

Brailsford is another master of his craft, with an open mind on learning from anywhere and an intense focus on every little detail that might affect performance. He has become associated with the concept of 'marginal gains', the idea being that the 100 small improvements one might make can actually add up to something that makes a measurable difference. Examples of marginal gains implemented by Brailsford included recognition that quality of sleep was an important factor for top athletes, but that the team had little control over quality of beds on the Tour de France, when staying in a different location every night. The solution: Team Sky bought their own mattresses and pillows, bespoke for each cyclist, and took them on the Tour with them.

Possibly a slightly more transferrable lesson started with the observation that there was a clear gap between time invested in meetings (high) and value of outputs (low). Brailsford instituted an outcome-driven approach, together with a new systemized format, to produce shorter, but better, meetings. No opportunity for performance improvement was missed. Brailsford clearly takes performance seriously, but was not above a little humour at the expense of some of the other teams in the Tour de France. He once told reporters that one of the outputs of his marginal gains programme was 'rounder wheels', something which was widely (and seriously) quoted, in particular in France, where a straight-talking Englishman's success in a historically French-dominated sport was not being well received.

Benchmarking (are you up for it?)

My own thoughts on the pursuit of excellence have been significantly influenced by my time as a pilot on the Red Arrows. The Red Arrows is a team in the truest sense of the word. It's not about one or two star individuals – a reasonable number of fighter pilots could probably reach the required standard. However, the team would generally be held up as an example of a high-performance team, in the United Kingdom and in many other countries, and so it is interesting to see what makes it tick. I will be delving more deeply into the team dynamic in the next chapter. For now, I just want to look at this issue of the pursuit of excellence in the widest sense. We have already had an insight into the micro issue of timekeeping, but what about the macro issues?

The first thing is that you need to have absolute clarity in what you are trying to achieve. Is it a case of beating some target or competitor? Hopefully most organizations can define a more meaningful goal than simply chasing a number; there is a limit to how excited one can get about that. What exactly are the Red Arrows trying to achieve? You could argue that they are in competition with the French, the Italians and the Americans – the other full-time professional national display teams. Is it a case of just being better than the others? Would that constitute success?

Actually the team is not just trying to be better than the competition; the aim is to be so much better that the other teams are irrelevant, to put clear blue water between them and the competition. That probably sounds arrogant and in no way reflects the day-to-day thinking on the team. The reality is that the other teams are very good indeed, do similar stuff to a similarly high professional standard and there is a strong mutual respect between the teams and the individuals on them. However, there is a serious point here. The Red Arrows run their own race. It is not a case of being a little bit better than someone else. The question is not how good are the competition, but how good could we be. What's the best possible standard that could be achieved? It's a bit like Google's thinking. They're no longer interested in a faster search time than some other search engine; it's more a case of trying to make the time infinitesimally short, to organize the world's information.

So what are the Red Arrows trying to achieve? The aim is perfection. And that is not some meaningless vision on a noticeboard somewhere. It actually means something: closeness to perfection is what is measured – all the shapes must be symmetrical with no timing gaps between manoeuvres and all 'the smokes' coming on and off at exactly the same time. Of course, true perfection is beyond the human and technical performance limits of the pilots and the aircraft. However, they can become good enough that it looks perfect from the ground. By aiming for perfection, near perfection can be achieved. If they aimed for very good, they would end up as good, if they aimed for good, they would end up as average, and if they aimed for average, they would end up as rubbish.

And the thing about aiming for perfection is that it's hard work – back to Syed and Gladwell. If you have an aim that is truly aspirational, beyond what other people are achieving, or what has been achieved before, then almost by definition that is going to be hard work. If it was easy, everybody would be doing it. There is rarely such a thing as overnight success, or at least one that stands the test of time; you normally just haven't seen the years of hard work that went in previously behind the scenes. You have to be ready to commit for the long haul.

When we talk about hard work here, that doesn't necessarily mean simply working very long hours, although in some cases it may do. It is probably true that many high performers have put in more time than their peer group. However, that's only part of the story. The other part is the intensity of focus, the relentless pursuit of truth and excellence;

it's hard work not just in the number of hours put in but in the standard you measure yourself against and what you regard as acceptable that can make the real difference. Never accepting anything other than excellence is hard work. In training with the Red Arrows, I used to fly three sorties a day, five days a week – fifteen sorties a week, each of which included a brief and debrief, and formed the backbone of a week that also included items such as the daily hosting of visitors, planning of the display season and PR activities, to name just a few. It was physically and mentally exhausting. It grinds you down, and you think that you will never be good enough. But that's what it takes. Excellence does not come cheaply.

My personal opinion is that the individual attitude to standards and the work ethic is one of the biggest barriers to the pursuit of excellence in large organizations. It's back to looking at yourself in the mirror: the issue is the standard you hold yourself to. What is 'good enough'? Is there such a thing? The Red Arrows hold themselves to a far higher bar internally than the one by which they are externally measured. The same is true of the New Zealand rugby team. I heard Sean Fitzpatrick (rugby World Cup winner and former All Blacks captain) speak with great passion and insight on the All Blacks' culture and what it meant to be an All Black. One of the themes was 'never being satisfied'. No matter how good the score or the game, there was always room for improvement. It's important to be able to recognize and celebrate success, but one can always do better. The question is whether you have the appetite for it. What standard are you prepared to hold yourself to?

The focus of this chapter is largely on the individual and when one looks at the sort of examples people tend to choose when asked about high-performance teams, the teams inevitably comprise individuals who want to be there, who are chosen by competitive selection. You have the luxury of choosing people with the right attitude. That will be a very difficult thing to replicate in organizations with thousands of people, many of whom work on low wages and might be there simply as a means of earning money to pay the bills. At that point the issue becomes not one of high-performance teams but of exceptional leadership, which we will explore in Chapter 7.

But we're creative

Hopefully much of what has just been said is self-evidently true. However, there are people who will be less than comfortable with this left-brained logical approach to life requiring a good dose of organizational skills and self-discipline. One client challenged me about the relevance of this approach for what was described as a 'creative' business. What this meant in practice for him was that 'creativity' was used as an excuse for being disorganized and an absence of discipline, but that needn't be the case, and discipline does not sit in opposition to creativity. Take for example the mindset of Bernaud Arnault, chairman of LVMH, a conglomerate comprising around fifty of the world's most powerful luxury brands. In an interview in 2001,[6] Arnault offered an interesting perspective on the dichotomy of managing creative superstars like John Galliano (before his fall from grace) at the same time as running a multi-billion dollar business. For him there was no conflict. Galliano must be completely unfettered by commercial and financial concerns to do his best work. However, creative industry or not, when it comes to the business of business, chaos is banished and the company undertakes meticulous planning, imposing a strict discipline on all aspects of the production and commercial processes. To scale creativity commercially, at some point, it needs to be 'operationalized'.

Summary of key points

- Excellence is not something achieved by association; it's about the standards, attitudes and behaviours which you personally bring to the party
- It's all about *you* – *your* behaviour will set the standard for those around you
- High performers always believe that they can go higher still
- High performers benchmark themselves against the best they could possibly be, not against the competition; they leave no stone unturned
- Creativity and rigorous discipline need not be mutually exclusive

The foundations

Chapter 3

Team players for team games (People)

Pte Luke Cole, 22, the Territorial Army soldier in Afghanistan who, despite being seriously injured, provided covering fire for his colleague and in the process was shot again during the night … said of his Military Cross: 'I am amazed. I was just doing my job.'

The private, a forklift truck engineer who was on a Territorial Army attachment with the Mercian Regiment, added: 'I didn't think I was doing anything special. I was helping my mates out like they would do for me.'

The Times, London, March 2008

Drivers of behaviour

Several years ago, Mission Excellence ran a series of team development workshops for the field sales force of a major pharmaceutical company. The challenge identified by the senior management was getting the sales representatives to buy in to the fact that success within the geographical sales teams was actually 'a team game'.

This concept of 'a team game' is itself worthy of comment. In *The Wisdom of Teams*,[1] Jon R. Katzenbach and Douglas K. Smith identify an important difference between teams and working groups. To paraphrase their idea, a working group is a group of individuals for whom the output is simply the sum of the efforts of the individuals. If all the sales reps work completely independently, and the total output cannot be improved beyond the sum of their individual outputs, then there is no point in pretending that they are a 'team'. They may well have common ground and some shared vested interests, but there is no significant degree of interdependence between them. The advantage of this approach is that you do not have to invest time and resources in team meetings, resolving conflict, and the organization and alignment of effort. In addition to being simpler, another advantage of the individual or working group approach is that people and organizations intrinsically prefer individual over team accountability; our ingrained individualism discourages us from putting our fates in the hands of others.

If, however, the task can only be achieved through cohesive effort, with individuals and sub-elements of the team being highly dependent on each other, then there is no alternative; you must make the *team* work. The lesson here is not to pretend to be teams, nor to try and force a team solution on a problem or environment that doesn't require it. Team working is a lot harder than just adding up the individual inputs, so there needs to be a clear benefit in going down this route. If a team approach is the right one, though, then the ability of the team members to work together effectively is likely to be a critical success factor.

Back at the pharmaceutical company, as part of the preparation for the workshop programme, I spent a day on the road with a sales rep, after which the senior training manager asked me for my perceptions of the working practices I'd seen. I think that she was slightly disappointed that my feedback ran to only three comments:

- You get the behaviour (performance) you train for.
- You get the behaviour (performance) you reward.
- Teams need leaders (or at least managers – somebody needs to be empowered and equipped to make decisions).

You get the behaviour (performance) you train for

In common with many pharmaceutical companies, this organization ran an induction programme that was based primarily on developing professional knowledge, dominated by data to support the efficacy of their drugs as compared to the competition, and sales skills. Reps were then put to work in a relatively complicated team environment. My concern was that you wouldn't send reps out to talk to doctors without equipping them with the professional knowledge and sales skills to do the job, so why would you expect them to be any good at team-working (a critical aspect of the role) without any training? However, behavioural development barely figured in the functionally dominated training programme.

Variations on this theme are manifold. I don't know how many employee feedback surveys we have seen that are coloured green (indicating positive feedback) all the way down from the top to first- or second-line management, and amber or red below (less positive or negative). First-line manager is repeatedly the point where things break down. Why is that? It's back to the same problem of functional competence versus behavioural attributes. That first critical promotion to manager is almost invariably based on functional performance – before you make first-line manager, there is often little or no opportunity to demonstrate management or leadership competency. However, the skills to lead the team are clearly different to the skills to be on the team. Why would the best engineer make the best team leader? The problem becomes particularly acute in professions that require high levels of specialist skill or intellectual ability, or where professional competence carries high kudos.

Some of the best examples on the issue of competence versus behaviour are provided in professional services and healthcare. Spending your life as a medical student always coming near top of the class, and then as a doctor, never really failing at anything, with significant social proof and reinforcement of your superior academic status could easily contribute to arrogance or some sort of superiority complex, where a surgeon accepts no challenge from others. This is not really a behaviour that I might want in the person carrying out a complex operation on me, no matter how skilled he might be.

We have done quite a lot of work with law firms, which also face a similar issue, compounded by the organizational set-up of many partnerships. People become lawyers for a myriad of reasons, almost certainly including a natural interest in the subject area, enjoyment of intellectual challenge, and attraction of the financial rewards. Junior lawyers want to become partners because then they will work on the biggest, most challenging cases, the role carries a lot of kudos, and you receive the highest remuneration. The reasons for wanting to be a partner do not necessarily include the desire to take on a wider management or leadership role, which is exactly what comes with the territory. Add to this a scenario where all the major shareholders come into the office every day (imagine running GE like that), the managing partner is often a first among equals and major decisions all require committee endorsement. This environment is going to have some leadership and management challenges.

The military solution is simple: to identify and develop future team players and leaders from day one, and to regard best-in-class functional competence simply as an essential requirement – something that goes with the territory. An individual may join because she wants to be a fighter pilot, but whether she likes it or not, she gets a thorough and career-long grounding in leadership and followership, and high performance against these criteria is essential for advancement. Officer first; pilot second.

Now I don't pretend that the military offers any perfect solutions and that there haven't been spectacular examples of poor military team effectiveness over the years. I also note that the various non-military sectors have produced many exceptional leaders who could have held their own in multiple fields, including the military. However, given the challenges of the environment, and the tasks involved, and having observed many commercial organizations over the last thirteen years, it is my belief that there are certain aspects of the military approach to non-technical skills and behaviours that deserve deeper consideration.

When I joined the RAF, my only ambition was to be a fighter pilot. But first I had to jump through a hoop called Officer Training. At the time, Officer Training was, to my mind, basically about polishing shoes, saluting, marching and running around carrying pine poles for four months (it has since been extended to eight months). It was simply something to be endured until I was able to start my flying training. However, in hindsight, I rationalize it rather differently. Before I even got my hands on an aircraft, I had to do this course on brand values, organizational history, the role of air power, leadership and teamwork. And only if I passed that course, would I get to learn any functional skills. As officers, leadership is what we do – that *is* the job. It doesn't matter how functionally brilliant you are; if you don't demonstrate the right behaviours, and leadership potential, you never even move beyond first base. And this theme of training in what might be called soft skills continues throughout your whole career. The investment of time, effort and resources in non-technical training and skill acquisition reaps rewards but the return may be difficult to quantify; it requires an intellectual leap of faith.

You get the behaviour (performance) you reward

However, equipping managers with the right behavioural traits and skills ultimately achieves no more than exactly that. As to what subsequently happens in practice, you get the behaviour (performance) you reward. Or, to put it another way, what gets measured gets done. This alignment of incentive with desired output seems so blindingly obvious, it's almost inconceivable that anybody could get it wrong. However, as pointed out by Stephen Kerr in his seminal paper, 'The Folly of Rewarding A, While Hoping for B',[2] organizations of every sort have been getting this wrong for a very long time (and continue to do so!).

The most common dichotomy in reward is between performance and behaviour. Investment banking is generally a good source of examples where an organization puts a heavy emphasis on the team franchise and a certain set of values in all its marketing promotion and recruitment, but ultimately only rewards financial performance. I remember a class discussion at business school dissecting a true case study of an issue faced by a managing director (MD) at one of the major investment banks. The problem was whether to promote a high-performing individual who was acting in a way that was in direct contravention of the values and behaviours espoused by the institution. I was forthright in my opinion that as the individual had had several warnings and chances already, the only credible answer to the promotion dilemma was 'no'.

I was pretty surprised by how many of the class held a more equivocal position. What was even more telling was that, after the debate, a colleague on the course for whom I had a lot of respect, and who worked in an investment bank, came over to chat about my comments. It wasn't so much that he disagreed; he simply didn't understand my perspective, and said that in his experience, the individual would be promoted every time.

The problem with this is twofold. If the values and behaviours that you are espousing as a senior leader really are that important, then the individual who is failing to adhere will ultimately drag the team down. Perhaps more importantly to you as a leader, he will also drag you down personally. The words coming out of your mouth will be seen to be meaningless, when someone who acts in direct contravention still gets promotion. In order to embed the 'right' behaviours, they must be routinely and consistently demonstrated by senior management, role models must be deployed, and there has to be public reward and recognition of those behaviours. You get the behaviour you reward.

Note that I am not saying that the investment bank mentioned would necessarily be wrong to promote the individual. It may be that behavioural issues are not that important, in which case let's not pretend otherwise and let's just revert to survival of the fittest and promote the winners; as long as you are honest about it, there's nothing fundamentally wrong with this. However, if behaviour is important, then as a leader, not only must you lead by example, you must also walk the talk when it comes to reward and recognition.

Jack Welch, a clear thinker of the highest order, brings some valuable insights to this subject in his book *Winning*.[3] He identifies four categories of performance:

- hits the numbers; right behaviours
- misses the numbers; right behaviours
- hits the numbers; wrong behaviours
- misses the numbers; wrong behaviours

Dealing with the first and last options in the above list is pretty easy: promote and fire, respectively. The second option is also not too demanding; that is someone you want on your team so you will invest some time and effort in coaching and developing that person to improve their performance level. The tricky one is the third option: someone who is delivering results, but not in the right way. Again, there is a case for coaching and development, but what to do if that fails? Sack a surefire winner? As we have seen earlier, my answer is an unequivocal yes.

For a common practical example of this misalignment of reward and behaviour, we return to the pharmaceutical sales teams described in the previous section. While senior management placed great store by the importance of team performance, bonuses were paid primarily on individual performance (it was actually subtly more complex – see later). So, if I am a very successful individual sales rep with years of experience, what incentive do I have to buy in to this 'team game'? My time would be better spent looking after my own interests.

Katzenbach and Smith identify 'mutual accountability' as one of their core prerequisites for high-performance teams. I couldn't agree with this more. Military and sports teams are often held up as examples of great teamwork; however, one thing which generally differentiates those teams from others is this issue of mutual accountability. Either everybody wins, or everybody loses. We are only measured by collective performance. Individual expertise is irrelevant if not translated into collective excellence (with apologies and thanks to Michael Thirkettle at McBains Cooper for the blatant reworking of his company's strapline).

I see a nice example of this individual versus team ethic in the TV programme, *The Apprentice*, where individuals try to impress a celebrity business mentor in a reality show, the prize for the winner normally being some sort of investment from, or role with, the mentor. In my opinion, the main reason for the success of this programme is the deliberate misalignment of incentives. Those who apply tend to be at least mildly narcissistic on a mission to self-promote and win an individual prize. However, all of the assessed tasks are team-based and, like any team-based activity, tend to be more successful if individuals adopt team-based behaviours. And there you have the recipe for reality TV success – teams that are dysfunctional by design.

Of course, the corporate world is rarely as neat and tidy as a football team or a military operation in measuring success. If mutual accountability is not intrinsic to the modus operandi, one easy way to generate it is through both financial reward and other measures of recognition, being tied to measures of performance apart from individual results. However, the complexities of large organizations, the inherent preference of individuals and organizations for individual, rather than team, accountability, and the misalignment of management's (short-term) interests with shareholders' (long-term) interests, make alignment of effort and reward somewhat more complex than meets the eye.

I used to think that the pharmaceutical company had actually done quite well in their bonus scheme. Although it didn't incentivise team performance, it was more complex than simply rewarding individuals. Any one rep's bonus would be a function of both individual performance and the company's performance. The company bonus level would define maximum bonus levels for the year, while the percentage of that which an individual actually received was defined by their annual assessment. If the company had a bad year, then no one got anything; if the individual performed badly, then they got a reduced sum, while other higher performers reaped greater rewards. I kind of liked this combination of individual and corporate assessment – you need to do a great job, but at the same time, we're all in it together.

The fallacy was punctured for me by Warren Buffet in Lawrence A. Cunningham's *The Essays of Warren Buffet*.[4] Buffet brings his usual clarity of thought to the issue of corporate reward and, while being a fan of collective performance assessment, believes that the principle only holds good to the level at which the individual can influence collective performance. Why should a team that has done brilliantly not reap the rewards, just because another part of the organization, over which they have no influence, has dragged down collective results?

The military solution to reward and recognition is, of course, also imperfect, not least through low levels of personal recognition – it's almost expected that you'll always do a great job to the best of your abilities. However, promotion, the most obvious form of recognition (and reward) in the military, is consistent with the philosophy underpinning recruitment and training. There is a heavy emphasis in all flying operations on leadership and the 'one team' aspect. In fact, the latter is so deeply embedded that it would be alien for an aircrew officer to think about it any other way. It's not about how good I can look, but all about delivering the external task. The armed forces operate no form of financial reward or bonus, and so the incentives are really around professional pride, personal satisfaction, and peer group credibility. Where these become somewhat more objective is in individual annual assessments, where in order to be in the bracket for promotion, one must be assessed as 'above average' both in professional competency, and in leadership (behavioural) attributes. It is simply not possible to be promoted on functional competence alone.

So having trained in leadership and behavioural traits, we need to reward and recognize the right behaviours in order to embed them as a reality in the organization. The issue of financial reward for business performance is probably the easiest example of misalignment to understand. There is however, a wealth of academic evidence that indicates the limitations of financial reward as a motivator;[5] it's a big hit for a few months, after which it's just what you get paid. Other forms of recognition may be equally or even more effective. Whatever form of reward and recognition is used, some things will always be true. You will get the behaviour you reward; what gets measured gets done.

Selection for the Red Arrows

The structures and processes which you can employ to make a team more effective tend to be well documented and pretty straightforward, even if not always so well implemented. However, my experience is that the real point of difference in small teams is not the *process*, but people's *attitudes*. By its very nature, teamwork requires team members to 'buy into the team game'. I find that the team dynamic and performance of the team will live and die with the attitude of the people within the team.

There are many examples of the great team successfully defeating the group of individual stars; sport provides some of the more obvious ones. The English Football Premier League has, in recent years, come to be the home of billionaire owners buying the best talent from around the world, yet the most consistent long-term performer of the last twenty years remains Manchester United, a team which is hardly poor but with less funding, and where the manager had a ruthless record of discarding stars who become too big for the team. The English national team sadly provides the opposite example, where some of the world's best talent has consistently failed to reach its collective potential as a team. So what is it that makes the difference?

The challenge for The Red Arrows

While the Red Arrows are often held up as an example of teamwork and excellence, the team faces some interesting challenges in terms of the team dynamic. Let me explain what I mean.

Imagine losing the most experienced third of your workforce each year, because that's what happens on the Red Arrows. There are about

100 people on the team, the 'front end' of which are the nine display pilots. And every year the three most experienced pilots leave, while the remaining six all change position, effectively changing their role on the team. Just think about that for a moment; this seems like the most stupid system and incredibly inefficient (only the military could think of it!). However, there are, of course, some good reasons for it: career progression, bringing in some fresh blood and certain operational factors. In fact, there are many positives that come from the churn, including fresh energy and ideas, and challenges to the status quo. But the interesting thing is that the display each year is just about always considered to be world-class, even though it's a different team. It's not about having one or two megastars. It's almost like the answer has been bottled; there's something in the culture, the behaviour, the 'how we do business around here' that can be reproduced year in, year out. Contrary to what my Mum told all the neighbours, I was not the hottest fighter pilot since Tom Cruise in *Top Gun*. Rather disappointingly, after I left, the team carried on producing the same great results without me.

So what are the things that are in the bottle? It starts with behaviour. I have presented many times on the subject of high-performance teams and I normally start by asking for examples of great teams and teamwork, and then asking people to think about the individuals on the team and what those people are like. What it is about them which makes the team so successful? Apart from the occasional completely wildcard response, the vast majority of answers come up again and again: drive, passion, focus, commitment, loyalty and so on. Now there's nothing there for most people to argue with – having a world-class team is about having people with those sorts of personalities.

Well, it is and isn't. It certainly can be those things, but you're not born passionate, focused and committed. You don't see six-month-old babies who are driven; these are behaviours and attitudes. You choose to make a commitment. You choose to make some personal sacrifices. There's clearly a bit more to it, but the bottom line is that you choose to be a world-class team. You definitely choose to be a team player. You choose a set of behaviours that align with the team agenda over and above a set of behaviours that align with pursuing your own. People may understand that issue but it's still human nature to question 'What's in it for me'? They actually make the commitment when the team goals are aligned with the personal goals; when they can see that delivering the team goals is the way to get the success, recognition, security, financial reward, esteem, or whatever it is that drives you personally. That's when they start to take ownership of the team goals and with that comes pride in what they are doing and a pride in the team. That's when they buy in. This is a very important concept – choosing a behaviour appropriate to the role or situation – choosing to be a team player. And it's a concept on which the military places a high premium.

The selection process

Even as a fighter pilot flying the Tornado, joining the Red Arrows was beyond my aspirations, and simply not 'on my radar'. It never occurred to me that this might be within the realms of the possible. I had never even met anybody on the Red Arrows until on one occasion I was doing some flying on the Tornado out in Cyprus, where there is a British base, and I got the chance to fly in the back seat of a Red Arrows practice display. I had already done a lot of formation flying so I thought I had a good idea as to what was reasonable in terms of proximity to other aircraft and proximity to the ground. The Red Arrows pilot who took me flying had a different perspective – it was all a bit of an eye-watering experience.

After the flight I attempted to have a conversation with the pilot without fawning too much, and in response to my pathetic drivel about how awesome it had been, he asked if I had applied to join. When I replied that I had not, he pointed out that you can't be selected unless you apply – if you don't go for something, you will never achieve it … which struck a chord with me and so I applied.

There is an annual selection process for which the team generally receives about thirty applications for the two or three pilots being replaced (the system is not quite symmetrical due to the fact that the Team Leader is one of the nine). The Team Leader has access to the candidates' flying records, added to which the RAF is not very big these days and so someone will almost certainly know the candidate (top tip for potential applicants: make yourself known to the current team!). The current pilots simply discuss the applicants with a view to forming a shortlist of nine. What you tend to be looking for at this stage is some combination of 'a good pair of hands' (i.e. decent basic flying skills) and people who are well thought of and respected by their peers.

When I applied, the fawning must have done some good because I made the shortlist of nine candidates. The final selection takes place during the Team's pre-season training in Cyprus (the Red Arrows normally train in southern Europe for a month or more at the end of the winter to 'guarantee' some good weather and continuity of training). The nine candidates come and join the Team for a week all at the same time. There are only three things that happen during that week: an interview (which takes all of 20 minutes), a flying test (another 20 minutes), and the final hurdle in selection for the Red Arrows ... socializing. A programme is put together that includes a variety of social activities and deliberately engineers a lot of interaction.

I can clearly remember my own experience on the shortlist week – the stress of the flying test, the being over-keen to impress, or sometimes feeling the need just to say something. However, it is perhaps more instructive to look at the process from the 'other side of the fence' – as a team member selecting new pilots.

I have always been of the opinion that the interview was pretty much a formality. Certainly when I was on the team, it was rarely a make-or-break item. In fact, I can only remember one person failing the interview. He was asked why he wanted to join the Red Arrows, a question which one might reasonably have predicted. And he responded that he quite fancied three years partying in a red flying suit. There's a time and a place for humour and that was probably neither.

The second part is the flying test. In my final year I was Deputy Team Leader, a role which includes conducting the candidate flying tests. What happens is that the Leader flies one jet and the Deputy (in this case, me) flies a second with the candidate in the rear seat of my aircraft (the Hawk is designed as an advanced trainer and so has a second seat behind the first with a full set of flying controls designed for an instructor). We taxi the two jets out onto the runway and take off together with my flying alongside the Leader's aircraft in close formation. Once airborne I ask the candidate if he can see the references I am looking at on the other jet to stay in formation. Hopefully they say 'yes' (it would be a short flying test otherwise!) and I hand control to the candidate and they take over the flying. The Leader then flies around eight aerobatic manoeuvres up and down the runway, one after the other. What I was looking for more than anything is smooth flying and the ability to demonstrate a learning curve. If the candidate is still making the same mistakes on the eighth manoeuvre as the first, then that doesn't bode too well for training. All in all, you're just looking to check that the core skills are in place.

One interesting thing I have noticed in presenting to audiences about high-performance teams is that when I ask about what the people are like on world-class teams, it's very, very rare that anybody mentions skills or functional excellence. And I would broadly agree with that omission. I'm not saying that those things are not important. The bar is set high in the flying test: it's 20 minutes of pure stress, but you pass it or you fail it – it's binary. The test is not the point of difference. Think of the test more like a line in the sand. You have to be on or over the line. Being a long way over is a good thing, but I can tell you from experience, that the team will always take somebody who is marginal on that line, but who is a great team player, over somebody who is brilliant but with an ego to match. Because that second person will drag the team down.

Which brings us on to the final part of the selection. The reason for taking the candidates away for a week is to try and find out what they are really like; it's very difficult to maintain a false image for a week. And what you are looking for comes back to the same things to which audiences always allude when I ask about the people on great teams: people who will choose to make the commitment and some personal sacrifices in support of the team agenda. You need people who understand that the team is always far bigger than any one star individual. And you need people you can trust.

What does trust actually mean? You don't choose to trust somebody or not; you just do. So why do you trust them? Think about your friends and colleagues; you trust some people more than others. Why is that? Well, you trust people who are honest. But what does that actually look like in a professional environment? People who do what they say they will, who deliver; people who, if they can't deliver, will let you know, so that you can manage it; people who can accept constructive criticism and feedback from their own peer group. And of course in the game of flying fighter jets, covering up your mistakes is not a matter of saving a few pounds or protecting your ego. It can have very, very serious consequences; people can die. So it's critical to get this right.

People tend to think that what the Red Arrows do is very technical or skills-based. But the selection process is about 90 per cent people-based. The talent pool is big enough; there are enough people who will pass the flying test. If you're playing a team game and everybody is competent, then the point of difference is generally not who is functionally better, but who has the right attitude? Who is choosing a set of behaviours that support the team's agenda and goals?

The challenge for senior leadership teams

As we will see in the next chapter, one interesting aspect of a fighter pilot mission is the issue of who leads it. You have different parts of a wide cross-functional team all operating under their own line management, often with a multinational make-up, where individuals might have limited or no formal line management authority across national boundaries. Who should be chosen to lead such a team? This is clearly a complex and messy scenario in the context of a legacy system of hierarchy and management through control. However, the answer to the leadership question is remarkably simple. The person who leads is the person best equipped to lead. What happens is that a lead group will be nominated, dependent on the nature of the mission; normally it will be chosen from one of the mission critical sections. Within that group, a suitably qualified and experienced individual will then be nominated as the mission commander. The interesting thing here is that the mission commander will not necessarily be the most senior person. So I can be flying as leader on this big mission as a junior officer in the British Forces, with a Saudi general and an American colonel on the same mission, but in the context of the mission they defer to me. We organize ourselves according to the external task, and are not limited by internal structure, or in this case hierarchy.

This might not sound such a big deal, and largely makes a lot of sense. However, think about the reality. My boss might be flying as 'number four' in my formation. Nothing changes the fact that he's still the boss and is the senior line manager. However, in the context of the mission he defers to me – something fairly extreme would have to happen for him to utilize his seniority while operating in the subordinate role. So the boss might arrive at work and come to ask me what needs doing. Basically as number four, he only has some minor responsibilities within the formation and is available to support others as required. With nothing specific to do, the boss might revert to making coffee or sandwiches for the rest of the formation. There is some interesting fallout from this concept: the boss gets regular practice at being in a subordinate role, at being *on* the team, rather than *leading* the team.

Contrast that with the concept of a senior leadership team – a group in which the inherent challenges in team effectiveness are often well illustrated. People form the senior leadership team with two 'hats on'. On the one hand, team members are generally some sort of functional head; they are present due to their role and responsibility as senior functional representative. However, as senior leadership team members they also have a collective responsibility for the performance of the whole business. The challenge herein is that the leadership role and the team player (or 'followership') role require a different set of behaviours; it's about *choosing a behaviour* appropriate to role.

The reality is that, apart from the CEO and perhaps one or two others who have a true organization-wide responsibility, those senior leadership team members spend about 95 per cent or more of their working days doing their leadership role in charge of their function; they're not getting a whole lot of practice in the team player role. Compounding this lack of practice is the fact that those people who made it that high in the organization are often alpha types, who far prefer the responsibility of running their functional area to the subjugation of personal interests and ego required of the team player. It's like politics – the traits you want in your ideal prime minister or president are often almost the opposite of the sort of traits it generally takes to get you there.

The output: a dysfunctional senior leadership team. I have seen more than a few examples of such team meetings, where individuals are clearly more interested in defending their own turf and scoring points at the expense of other functional heads than they are in collectively owning and addressing the wider business issues.

The underlying challenges in senior team effectiveness are often no more complex or different to teams at any other level – solutions at all levels include equipping people with the required non-technical skills, and aligning effort and reward. You are often just dealing with stronger personalities. However, when it does happen, dysfunction in the senior leadership team can have a significant impact on the whole organization. It takes a particularly high level of emotional maturity and intelligence to be able to take a purely objective perspective on what would be best for the organization, without reference to, and indeed perhaps at the expense of, any personal consequence for my own functional area. Objectivity is a consistent theme and driver of excellence throughout this book and we will explore it more deeply in Chapter 6.

Team banking – a case study

Our client was a wealth management company. The structural set-up was that private bankers (PBs) were formed into both client sector and regional teams, with each PB having their own client list. When a new MD took over the role, the business was clearly living on past glories and significantly underperforming against its potential. Before describing any further detail of the actions taken, I should point out that we can take only limited credit for the success described here – the key elements of the development strategy were already worked out by the MD before we were engaged to support it.

The first step taken by the MD was to introduce formal performance management for PBs. That alone produced a marked improvement, but with bonuses ultimately capped, its effect was finite. So he uncapped bonuses. This had a predictable motivational effect, but with only 24 hours in the day, and seven days in the week, the effect was still finite. And as already pointed out, a pay rise simply moves the expectation bar. Furthermore, the MD started to wonder if the fundamental concept of a sole trader model with PBs running individual client lists might be flawed.

First, he wondered if a well-organized team might be able to actually service more clients than the sum of the individuals; not least it would introduce redundancy and mutual cross-cover, for example, for leave and sickness. Second, financial services products had become increasingly complex in recent years, and so it was near impossible for any single PB to have in-depth expertise across all relevant professional areas. However, since her bonus was determined largely by funds under management from her clients, there was little incentive for the PB to introduce one of her colleagues with more relevant professional expertise for a particular issue, or for the colleague to offer her time for that purpose. Finally, when a new PB joined a team, there was almost no incentive for PBs to spend time developing the new team member or to transfer any valuable clients to the new team member.

So the MD decided to introduce 'Team Banking'. PB teams would share a common client list across the team in order to address all of the factors just mentioned. The initial reaction of many PBs was extremely negative. A few stars immediately jumped ship to competitors, who they thought would better compensate their individual talents, while many of those remaining were vociferous in their opposition. However, a pilot scheme gave grounds for optimism. After 18 months the new system was fully embedded, with PBs increasingly committed to the team ethos. Client feedback was extremely positive and all relevant business performance measures improved over that time period.

Why did it work? The key to success was overt and proactive executive sponsorship. Team Banking became the common theme in all internal communication, providing constant positive reinforcement. Most importantly though, directors and senior managers were trained in leading teams, while PBs and Private Banking Assistants (PBAs) were trained in team working, including facilitation of individual team effectiveness workshops. And the reward system was changed to recognize the importance of team-based behaviours. The legacy sole trader system of individual bonuses was replaced by a bonus system based on individual performance, team performance and the results of 360-degree feedback. It would perhaps have been a step too far to completely remove the individual element, but one should not underestimate exactly how big a change it was to have any element of collective performance and behavioural assessment in the bonus calculation. The use of 360-degree feedback in this context is actually fairly contentious – using development tools for assessment purposes is strongly discouraged in HR circles (the impact of feedback on pay is highly likely to skew the objectivity of the process, and therefore dilute the value). However, it did make a clear statement of intent – what gets measured gets done.

The MD deployed some other trump cards during the change process. One was to put one of the loudest cynics in charge of the pilot scheme. When this proved a great success, the former cynic was then utilized as a highly credible and influential internal champion. And the MD also included PBAs within the reward scheme. The effect of the latter was immediate and dramatic. During the pilot scheme phase, when the MD visited the legacy teams, it was business as usual with PBAs simply getting on with the job as normal. When he visited the pilot scheme teams, he noted that when a PB came into the office, the reaction of the PBA was to kick her back out to go and earn some revenue. The PBA now had a far higher vested interest in the PB's contribution to the team effort.

It is difficult to accurately portray the scale of cultural and organizational change which occurred in this client; it had been doing business using the sole trader model for more than 100 years. However, a combination of executive sponsorship, 'over-communication', deployment of role models and, most importantly, training and rewarding the right behaviours, produced a dramatic transformation in less than eighteen months. The core lessons apply across the spectrum from the development of first line managers and teams, to the dynamics of senior leadership teams.

Developing the high-performance team – processes

You can lead a horse to water but you can't make it drink. You can do everything possible to embed the right team-based values and behaviours, and you can perfectly balance individual and team incentives to reward the 'right' behaviours and performance outcomes, but some teams are still remarkably more effective than others. What's the difference?

It is worth considering the question: When does great teamwork happen? Well, this might seem a rather trite answer, but it happens when it's required. Incredible examples of teamwork sometimes emerge with little or no conscious decision or training, simply because great teamwork is the only way to resolve a situation, for example, in a survival situation following an aircraft crash. In a hospital operating room, there is no financial incentive to adopt a team working model and staff may have received little or no formal training in team working. However, team members routinely deliver outstanding collective performance because that is the only way to save the patient's life.

Consider these four examples:

- A HEMS (Helicopter Emergency Medical Services) helicopter is dispatched to the scene of a major incident in order that medical support can be provided to a critically ill patient.
- A turnaround team is 'parachuted in' to take control of a business that will run out of cash in twenty days.
- A military special forces team is inserted to carry out a dangerous hostage rescue.
- An international sports team lines up in the World Cup final.

What are the common features, in the context of team dynamics, that bind all these examples together? The most important is *task clarity*, without which we are on a near certain path to mediocrity. *What specifically are we trying to achieve and why?* The answers to this question can be deceptively difficult to reach. In the preceding examples, they should be relatively simple:

- Stabilize the patient in order to get them to hospital.
- Generate positive cashflows in order to buy time to protect investor funds (there may be much wider issues at play – for example, to save jobs – but the turnaround team will have most likely been brought in by debt or equity holders).
- Rescue the hostage in order to remove them from a threat to their life.
- Win the game in order to become world champions.

These examples are helped by being self-evident, time-bounded 'missions', but what of 'business as usual'? It is going to be very hard to provide direction and motivate people unless the long-term goals can be broken down into similarly discrete tasks that have outcomes. We worked with a senior leadership team from a county council who set themselves the unenviable task of trying to define what it was that bound them together as a team. You may think that the answer should be obvious, but they were working on cross-functional projects with a variety of dependent and independent responsibilities. Add in a range of ambiguous political imperatives and long-term projects sponsored by politicians with short-term time horizons, and you can start to see the challenge.

However, without clarity, what should people actually do at work? What are the priorities for resourcing decisions in the short and medium term? We spent the best part of two days getting to an answer to just two related questions: 'what' [are we trying to achieve] and 'why'– that is, achieving clarity. The value of that investment of time and effort in answering such a simple question was crystal clear to the deputy chief executive: '… clarity in the "main effort" underpinned a culture shift across the entire organization. People now understand what their focus should be every day that they come to work.'

The next feature that is highly likely to be present in the four previous examples is *role clarity*. Everybody understands their contribution to the team effort, why it is important and how it relates to other people's roles. We thereby introduce specialization and focus of effort, and eliminate duplication of effort. Ownership of a role is also a significant motivator; the team is relying on me to get this contribution right.

With clarity in who is doing what, when and why, we are now best placed to optimize the allocation of resources (including time – often the scarcest resource of all). And with all that in place, and everybody understanding exactly what is expected of them, what should the team leader do? The answer again is both simple and deceptively difficult: lead. What we mean by that word will be discussed in Chapter 7, but for now a more accurate and simpler substitute word is 'manage'. Unless the team is engaged in some task that is particularly demanding, inspirational leadership, while always welcome, is unlikely to be required. However, somebody has to set the direction, allocate the initial roles and responsibilities, and 'hold the hammer' on the allocation of resources. If the team is new, then they will require detailed direction and guidance. If the team is already well established and well drilled, then a hands-off approach is likely to be more effective. The team knows what to do. The manager's job then is to provide context and goal setting – to be a 'light hand on the tiller' rather than micromanaging.

You cannot make people into great teams simply because you legislate it so. However, for those who would like to see some academic rigour to underpin the observations above, Katzenbach and Smith identify four factors that they found common to many true high-performance teams – putting these factors in place should definitely maximize the chance to develop such teams (my words in italics):

- Clarity in common purpose – *'Why'*
  This is the context or direction – the higher intent which we are contributing to or working towards. Some may prefer the word 'vision'. A powerful vision can be truly inspiring, however one has to be certain that a vision does actually have meaning and relevance. I prefer the simpler 'why' rather than getting too hung up on artificially trying to craft a vision.
- Performance goals – *'What'*
  Intent needs to be translated into measurable and accountable tasks that, if achieved, will deliver that intent.
- Common approach – *'How'*
  An agreed method of working, and direction towards the performance goals, which all team members are employing (you can't just do your own thing!); this will implicitly include role clarity and allocation of resources.
- Mutual accountability
  Collective measurement of performance – 'you all live and die together', or to put it another way, you get what you reward; if it's a team game, make the team collectively accountable.

One of the reasons I like Katzenbach and Smith's model, apart from the refreshing absence of psychobabble, is that it relates very accurately to some of my own experiences in teams as a fighter pilot and on the Red Arrows. In that world, the last item in this list is one we don't even think about. Doing an individual great job is irrelevant if we don't achieve the mission. Flying your jet perfectly is irrelevant if the show is not perfect. It's the same in sports teams – individual brilliance is irrelevant if the team loses. In the commercial world, it is of course possible to set this up artificially to some extent, simply by measuring people on collective performance.

Katzenbach and Smith identified that it is when the four factors above are present that you get a 'real team' which is functioning effectively as a team. However, they also identified a fifth factor that moves the team up the performance curve (they are management consultants, after all) from a 'real team' to a 'high-performing team' once the four main criteria are all in place: team members who are deeply committed to one another's personal growth and success. I can see the sense in this, and the authors conducted extensive research on the subject; however, I am not certain from my own experience that it is a prerequisite. When the task is intrinsically highly challenging and rewarding, and it can only be achieved through a team effort, then I believe that their fifth criterion in achieving high performance is desirable rather than essential. The team will raise their game anyway.

However, I did like the concept of the whole team moving up and down this performance curve together. The Red Arrows finish their summer display season almost certainly as a high-performing team by any sensible benchmark. Then the three most experienced pilots leave and three new pilots join. So do the three new pilots have a daunting task in moving up to the high-performing standard of everyone else? No, because if you are measured collectively as a team, then the whole group must re-form as a new team further down the performance curve and collectively move back to a high-performing level. This is the essence of mutual accountability and the team game.

Summary of key points

- You get the behaviour you train for:
  - Training only in functional competence will not deliver team players or leaders
  - The best functional performers will not necessarily make the best managers and leaders
  - Train in non-technical as well as technical skills from day one

- You get the behaviour you reward:
  - What gets measured gets done
  - As a leader, you *must* reward and recognize the right behaviours; *and* deal with the wrong behaviours
  - If it's a team game, make the team mutually accountable
  - Reward collective performance only up to the level at which it can be influenced
  - If promotion means wider leadership responsibility, then make leadership performance a prerequisite
- Senior leadership teams:
  - Leaders must choose a behaviour appropriate to role
  - Instil objectivity and collective responsibility in top teams
- Developing high-performance teams:
  - Task clarity (and context) – what are we trying to achieve and why
  - Role clarity – who will do what when
  - Allocation of time and resources
  - Effective team management – context, direction and a light hand on the tiller – step in only for new teams or by exception

Chapter 4

Building the teams and organization you need (Capability)

We trained hard, but it seemed that every time we were beginning to form up into teams we would be reorganized. I was to learn later in life that we tend to meet any new situation by reorganizing, and a wonderful method it can be for creating the illusion of progress, while producing confusion, inefficiency, and demoralisation.

Caius Petronius, AD 66

Britain's worst customer service company? (a hotly contended title!)

It is not unusual for a significant gap to exist between the service experience which a company aspires to deliver and what happens in practice. Consider this example from my own experience of dealing with my former business bank. We had originally opened an account with the Commercial Banking department some years previously. At some point, the account management was moved without my knowledge to a different manager in a different department and location, although our nominal branch remained the same. For reasons that I never understood, our credit card account was set up through a partner bank; there appeared to be no commonality between the internet and telephone banking systems for our current and credit card accounts. The internet banking service only allowed me to move £20,000 per day, however even that became problematic when my card reader (security system for online transactions) ran out of power. And I couldn't arrange certain tranfers through telephone banking, or make an international transfer either online or by telephone since a letter or face-to-face authorization was required. Almost no part of the service offering was integrated with any other and nothing about it was customer-centric.

Faced with a need to make an international transfer one day, I went into a branch at lunchtime to complete the process in person. But of course the manager had sent the staff for lunch at the busiest time of the day. With one cashier working, I waited 20 minutes. Eventually I got to the front of the queue, to be told that the cashier couldn't deal with my request and that I needed to queue again for the 'front of house' person, who was possibly the least helpful service representative I have ever met. I gave up and left without managing to organize the transfer.

In parallel to my rather ineffective visit, I had requested a new card reader online but nothing had been received. With no internet option available to move money, I called telephone banking to organize some transfers I needed to make, and to order a new card reader. But they couldn't just press a button to order a card reader; it was the job of a different department. The service assistant suggested ordering online! After I explained that I had already tried that, he transferred me to the card reader ordering department. It turned out that they held an old address for the business, even though all routine correspondence was received at the correct address. So I asked the new assistant to change the address, but he said that I would need to speak to yet another different department. I hung up.

Now it seems unlikely that a senior manager had sat down with the express aim of designing a completely dysfunctional, disconnected service experience. If they had, they had done an outstanding job. But that was undoubtedly the end result. Equally, it seems unlikely that the individuals who dealt with me had woken up that morning with the clear intention to make their customers' lives difficult and to engage in adversarial conversations. But that's how it felt. If we start from the assumption that they weren't trying to have that effect deliberately, then the problem appears to be that, for some reason, they had not been given the tools or the permission to provide the seamless service that is exactly what they would want if they were the customer. In fact, it was quite the opposite. They had been given a task and constraints that implicitly made it impossible to serve a customer in the way in which the customer wants to be served. And in fact, it is often not even their job to do that. At the most basic level, the job is often to deal with customer issues, in compliance with internal systems. *Compliance and activity are what get measured, not successful outcomes or satisfied customers.* Remember from Chapter 3 that you will get what you reward, and that what gets measured gets done.

How does the gap become so large between the service experience that a company aspires to deliver and what it actually delivers in practice? Where does the organizational design and process go wrong? Large organizations are generally quite complicated, with individuals and teams often working as part of extended virtual or matrix networks. Sometimes people have little or no direct contact with other team members and report simultaneously through a functional line management chain at the same time as an operational task management. Either functional or operational line management might be the primary channel in terms of career management, which will definitely influence where a person's primary focus is.

As an example, if I am a corrosion engineer in an oil company, I might simply report to the head of the oil rig on which I operate, or I might report to the head of corrosion (who does not work on my specific rig), and just be deployed to the rig, with the head of the rig having limited line authority over my work. There is no right way to do this and there are pros and cons to both of these scenarios.

Whatever the system employed, it is invariably designed from the perspective of internal cost and efficiency, whereas the customer is only interested in the effectiveness of the system in addressing their own (external) problems. Aligning interests and working practices, and sharing information effectively can be extremely difficult in the sorts of systems just described and can lead to exactly the sort of scenario I described with my former bank. This chapter outlines some solutions to the challenge of building the capability to be highly effective in teams and organizations.

When talking about people and behaviours in the last chapter, it was useful to focus on the personal interactions intra-team. When talking about capability, the principles are similar within a single team or a large organization; however, in the latter case, the scale of the communication and alignment challenges multiplies significantly, so that is the main focus of this chapter.

Britain's best team?

I also came across a rather different example of the effect of an organizational system on individual performance. We have done some work within the UK National Health Service (NHS), through which I became friendly with one of the senior managers (who is also a clinician). He was invited to visit the military medical facilities at Camp Bastion in Afghanistan to observe clinical practices 'in the field'. On the first day, he was incredibly impressed by the energy, focus, can-do attitude and professionalism of the military clinicians, which resulted in highly effective working practices. On the second day, he was very proud to realize that a majority of the personnel were actually only part-timers in the military and were in fact NHS staff. On the third day, the penny dropped. Why don't we see this same attitude on NHS time? Clearly, it wasn't the people; they were the same people! He knew that the NHS was full of committed, talented people who did an amazing job every day, but there was something about the environment at Bastion which took performance to a new level. What was the difference? Set them free in the right environment with a clear mandate and purpose, and the right tools and permission to get on with it, and the output was exceptional.

To consider a different way of thinking about cross-functional teams in large organizations, I would like to return to my first career and consider the example of a fighter pilot mission. If you have any doubts about whether fighter pilot missions are the relevant analogy for your team, there is a quote from James Dewar which is very relevant at this point: 'A mind is like a parachute; it works better when it is open.' I hope that whatever your view on the relevance of the military analogy, you will find the model interesting.

Learning to be a fighter pilot

Life as a fighter pilot is pretty much a continuous learning curve, not least in teamwork and leadership. In flying training, first one learns the core functional skill, to fly and navigate a basic training aircraft. Then one hones those skills on a faster and higher performance jet trainer, and just when you think you're getting somewhere, rather disappointingly, the baseline is completely redrawn. From the point at which you get your 'wings' and become a qualified RAF pilot, it is more or less taken as read that you know how to take off, land and fly aerobatics, can do basic formation flying and navigate from A to B, and those aspects are no longer really assessed to the same extent.

The new baseline is to operate the aircraft, to do something with it, both as a wingman and leading someone else. The next phase of training culminates in an assessed sortie, where you lead your instructor (who acts as the wingman) on a training mission flown at 250 ft and 420 kts (approx 500 mph or 800 kph), with two targets to attack, each within a 10 second timing bracket, while simultaneously reacting to and defending yourself against simulated attacks from another instructor in an aircraft playing the role of the enemy fighter.

Then the baseline is completely redrawn and you move on to a frontline high-performance fighter aircraft. After perhaps four months training to fly the fighter jet, and most likely at least two and a half years total in flying training, you finally arrive on your first fighter squadron, fully qualified ... to do almost nothing. Because then the baseline is completely redrawn.

A further four to six months in your squadron sees you qualified as 'combat ready' as a wingman, effectively flying as the junior team member in small teams. And so it continues, qualifying as a leader of those teams and flying as a wingman in larger inter-team missions with different types of aircraft from other squadrons, over time learning to lead ever larger missions.

Putting the training to the test

When I stood up in the main auditorium at Nellis Air Force Base in Nevada, USA, I had received four months of dedicated training in leadership, followership and organizational values (officer training), two and half years of functional skill training learning to fly and operate a jet, and three years on-the-job training of daily intra- and inter-team activities, each thoroughly debriefed to accelerate the resultant learning. If I was in a better place than Caius Petronius (quoted at the start of this chapter), it was not an accident. In front of me at Nellis, fifty aircrew from four nations represented by seven different squadrons, waited to hear the air defence brief for that night's strike mission. Together with my weapons systems officer, I would be leading eight Tornado and six F-16 fighters protecting six Harrier and four B-1B bombers who were carrying out a night attack on an enemy HQ and logistics centre. The enemy territory would be defended by ten F-18 Hornet fighters and a variety of ground-based missile systems with the potential to really ruin your evening.

The time was now 19.00 and in approximately two hours, twenty-four fast-jet aircraft together with a wide range of supporting aircraft and crews would take off into the worsening night weather to execute a complex and dangerous high-speed game of aerial chess. Clearly, safe and successful execution would require a well-drilled experienced team to act in perfect cohesion. Unfortunately, my own team of Tornado crews was a completely random selection from our squadron, and we had never even met any of the other crews before the previous day, let alone worked together. However, this was not a time for whining or excuses. This was what we trained for. This was war.

Well, not exactly. This was actually Exercise Red Flag, possibly the closest that a fighter pilot can come to the experience of going to war without doing it for real. Red Flag is an exercise hosted and managed by the US Air Force, primarily out of Nellis Air Force Base in Nevada. Its purpose is to provide a highly realistic simulation of wartime operations, and was developed as a result of mixed US results in air combat in Vietnam.

In spite of an apparent technological advantage, the ratio of kills to losses in Vietnam was significantly less than in previous wars, with many aircraft also lost to ground-based missile systems. Subsequent analysis showed that air force training had come to be dominated by long-range missile encounters, and that pilots were relatively under-trained for close-in visual combat. Furthermore, there was clear evidence indicating that survival rates increased with mission experience, with ten combat missions identified as a nominal tipping point. So Exercise Red

Flag was developed in the 1970s in order to offer US, NATO and other allied aircrews the opportunity to fly simulated combat missions with measurable results in a safe training environment. Exercise Red Flag is the closest that crews can get in peacetime to flying those ten missions.

The Nellis airspace covers an area of approximately 6,000 square miles, within which large multinational packages can perform a variety of simulated combat missions. The 'enemy' is provided both by other 'friendly forces' operating in that role (e.g. another allied squadron), in addition to dedicated 'aggressor' squadrons with pilots who are specifically trained in the tactics of likely aggressors. Ground-based missile threats are provided both through synthetic simulation and the use of actual acquired and captured 'enemy' systems. Electronic monitoring of all aircraft within the range and the live download of the use of their weapons systems mean that missions can be reconstructed and analysed in detail, in order to extract individual and collective lessons on performance and effectiveness.

Returning to my own mission at Red Flag, in order to help understand the dynamics of the cross-functional challenge, what I'd like to do is to build a generic mission team, as shown in Figure 4.1, and then to examine the drivers of successful mission execution for the sort of task we faced that night.

Building the teams you need

The first step is simply the definition of the mission. This may or may not sound obvious but the importance of that statement should not be underestimated. I will return to this point later; however, the start point is the thing to be achieved. The first element of the team to be added will be the mission critical bit, the element that has to deliver.

This might be the strike force of bomber aircraft employed to destroy some critical installation, the special forces inserted covertly by helicopter, or perhaps the humanitarian aid delivered from transport aircraft. The role of everybody else is not to do their own functional job in isolation, but to support the mission critical element. The whole point of the mission is for the mission critical element to deliver an outcome.

Figure 4.1 The mission team

The next factor to consider is the defence of the mission critical element against attack from other aircraft or ground-based systems. The job of the air defence fighters is to go out first and engage with the enemy fighters, to make the airspace a safe place for everybody else to operate in; typically in modern operations, nobody else moves until air supremacy, or at least superiority, has been established. Other similar elements engaged in offensive support roles include SEAD (Suppression of Enemy Air Defences). The role of SEAD aircraft (normally some sort of fighter themselves) is to neutralise ground-based missile systems.

Alongside all of the factors just mentioned – the mission critical element and the offensive support aircraft – there will almost always be an essential requirement for live intelligence updates, coordination and communication for the mission. You may remember that 'no plan survives first contact with the enemy'. This issue is addressed by an AWACS aircraft (the old Boeing 707 with the radar dish on top) or one of the more modern similarly equipped aircraft. Its crew's job (among other things) is to build what is called the 'Recognized Air Picture', that is, a live picture of everything that is happening in the operating environment, how the mission is evolving and to keep all crews updated on the relevant aspects of that picture. The execution is never a flawless replication of the plan and the AWACS facilitates the collision of the plan with reality, in real time.

The communication element of the role is examined later in the chapter. For now, it is sufficient to note that there is a central node that constantly collates all the sources of intelligence, monitors the 'mission dashboard', and disseminates relevant updates to those who need them. The AWACS is an extremely effective live feedback loop or knowledge management system. While the mission commander will normally be part of the mission critical element, the AWACS crew also has a critical role in providing the link to higher authority where required, and in many cases providing permission for engagement. The AWACS is the communications node for the mission. To provide some context of the importance placed upon this role, the AWACS would often be considered mission critical – if the AWACS is unserviceable, the mission is postponed.

The next element within the make-up of the mission are the air-to-air refuellers. They are what we call a force multiplier. For example, instead of needing three groups of fighters, we can use two but stay airborne longer by refuelling. Instead of only being able to fly 300 mi, we can fly 1,000. And the mission will be completed by the addition of any number of support elements. I have just included combat search and rescue and intelligence as examples here.

Making the connection between this sort of mission and a non-military mission may require a little artistic licence; however, consider the model that follows at Figure 4.2.

At the centre is some sort of brand target to be achieved by sales and key account managers. Marketing goes out there first and prepares the way for everybody else. Coordination and communication is provided (hopefully!) by the senior leadership team. IT systems provide a number of force multipliers, for example, Customer Relationship Management, while finance, HR and any number of shared resources form critical support elements. I know we're simplifying things here,

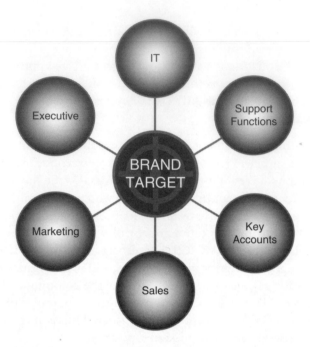

Figure 4.2 The corporate mission

but the point is that contrary to popular misconceptions about the military and hierarchy, your average fighter pilot routinely faces exactly the sort of cross-functional challenges that exist in many commercial organizations. And they have to be resolved in an environment where mistakes cost lives.

There are a number of interesting features about this mission model. The first is that it is a team. It might not fit almost any of the criteria used to define a team on training courses where often teams can only consist of a small number of people (fewer than ten?) and must fit various other criteria in order to be described as a team. This group has at least fifty people in it and maybe 1,000 in the extended group; however, I would argue absolutely that this is a team. No one person or sub-group can achieve the task in isolation. Only by the whole extended group acting interdependently and in cohesion towards a single aim can the outcome be delivered.

Possibly the most interesting thing about this team is that it is wholly driven by the mission, by getting the job done. In commercial terms, it is completely market- or environment-centric as opposed to being process- or product-centric. The starting point is not our internal structure, but what the end result looks like, and then what resources are needed and how must they be organized in order to achieve that end result. The thinking is very much 'effects-based'. We are less interested in how we get there than simply that the mission is delivered in the most effective way possible. To that end we put together the right team to get the job done, and that will probably involve slicing across local hierarchies, functions and locations.

An excellent example of this is to highlight the issue previously mentioned (when talking about senior leadership teams in Chapter 3) of who leads this mission. I might be the leader without being the most senior person. But in the context of the mission, seniority is not the key issue; the person who leads is the best equipped to lead. People tend to have a perception of the military as very hierarchical. In line management, it absolutely is; you know exactly where you stand. He or she who has the highest rank gets saluted the most. However, in military aviation, there's too much at stake to be making decisions based solely on ego and rank. Of course, this doesn't change the fact that the senior line manager is still the senior line manager, but something exceptional would have to happen for him to exert that authority in the context of the mission.

Building capability in the team

Structuring the mission team is one thing. But how do you get it to actually work as one cohesive unit and not result in the disconnected silos that I saw in the bank? And don't forget that this is complicated. The reality here might be seventy aircraft taking off from different bases with crews of different nationalities from different cultures, who have never worked together before, never met, maybe even never spoken; they have just coordinated remotely. And yet they need to get it right first time. In bad weather. At night. With people trying to stop them. This is the ultimate competitive environment.

Also, remember that this is not simply an exercise in exceptional planning and organization. As I pointed out in Chapter 2, many of the variables are outside our control. You are highly reactive to the 'bad guys', the environment and all the factors, including good and bad luck, which might affect your own team. In short, in spite of the number of players and complexity of the task, we need to have the agility to change the plan and execution as the situation evolves in real time.

I talk in more detail about safety and risk management in Chapter 8, however, as a general principle, neither safety nor agility are separate issues to execution itself; they are both an essential requirement and a natural by-product of how we do business. Agility in particular is highly correlated to empowerment. When clients approach Mission Excellence with an interest in how to be more agile, I often think that they have framed the wrong question; they should be asking about leadership. Agility is not a box you can tick in isolation.

So how does it actually work? Well, you can guarantee that if your average fighter pilot needs to understand it, it's not going to be rocket science. Agile execution boils down to three core issues:

Clarity – Alignment – Empowerment.

Clarity

Clarity in common purpose is really the first step in achieving alignment of effort; however, it is of such importance that we break it out as a separate issue. In fact, if I was going to sum up in one word the most fundamental barrier to high performance that we observe, it would be poor clarity: task clarity, role clarity and, maybe most important of all, clarity in common purpose. You will remember my previous comment about employee engagement surveys showing a lot more 'red' at lower levels in the organization. In the critical customer-facing, service delivery or product manufacturing roles, many people simply have no visibility on why they do what they do, or what the organization is trying to achieve and why.

If our cross-functional team includes people in different locations, working in different line managements, possibly in different time zones, with different commitments, and maybe levels of commitment to this particular task, then it's clearly not going to be possible to micromanage them; it is absolutely vital that they are all 'singing from the same sheet'. The following is a quote from *Alice's Adventures in Wonderland*, a British children's fairytale that illustrates nicely what happens when there is no clarity on where we are trying to go:

Alice (to the cat): 'Would you tell me which way I ought to walk from here?'
The cat: 'That depends a good deal on where you want to get to.'
Alice: 'I don't care much where.'
The cat: 'Then it doesn't matter which way you walk.'

A slightly more practical example is contained in the following example, which used to be on a sign outside a base I flew from in the RAF (it's not there any longer – possibly a bit too direct and politically incorrect for the twenty-first century?):

The job of this base is to fly and fight
The job of those that don't is to support those that do
Everyone is an aviator

Everyone is an aviator … Everyone is in sales … Everyone is in customer service … You might argue that at some level this is a simplistic piece of jingoism and I couldn't disagree with you. But at another level it is quite a nice example of simple clarity in common purpose. A thousand people a day would walk past that sign and be reminded that the reason we go to work is to put fighter aircraft in the air. For the young eighteen-year-old who manages requests for leave in the headquarters, his job is not just about compliance with administrative processes, filling in spreadsheets or shuffling paper around; it's about freeing up the pilots' time to put jets in the air. My role as a fighter pilot was not about simply taking on the opposition's fighters; it was about delivering the mission. Possibly the most famous (apocryphal?) example of collective buy-in is the story of the cleaner at NASA who was asked what his job was; he replied: 'To put a man on the moon.'

Alignment

Common sense says that if you want bank staff to solve customers' problems, or for fighter pilots to change the plan in the heat of the moment, then they have to be empowered to do so. But you can't empower without alignment first. The result would be chaos. Assuming that we have clarity in common purpose, alignment is driven by three further factors: commitment to that purpose, a common approach and communication. Commitment describes the emotional buy-in to the task or cause; a common approach and communication process are practical drivers of alignment.

Commitment

There is no more powerful lever in driving commitment than leadership, and there are several leadership facets that will combine to drive engagement.

We have already covered the first: clarity in common purpose. In general, humans thrive on purpose; it provides meaning and focus. However, *defining* purpose is only half the story. There is also a requirement to *communicate* purpose; motivation and engagement will likely be driven by some combination of a powerful and meaningful intent communicated in simple terms with passion. And the communication needs to be repeated and backed up symbolically through leaders' behaviours and personal commitment to the purpose. What the leader says is one thing, but what people really notice is what leaders *do*. When you reach a senior executive position, it's very easy to forget how you noticed and monitored senior leaders' actions and behaviours yourself, when you were in a more junior role. When you find yourself in that position, you're just the person you always were in your own mind, and you forget that younger, more junior people view you very differently. The symbolism of your behaviour can have an enormous impact. Consider the quote below from Carlos Ghosn, simultaneously chairman of both Renault and Nissan (the bold highlighting is mine):

> *I think that the best training a top manager can be engaged in is management by example. I want to make sure there is no discrepancy between what we say and what we do. If you preach accountability and then*

*promote somebody with bad results, it doesn't work. I personally believe the best training is management by example. **Don't believe what I say. Believe what I do.***

Clarity can be improved by clear consistent and repeated articulation. However, in order for people to believe and act on the communication, whether it be purpose, values or priorities, they need to see senior executives 'walk the talk' themselves.

Next, we move to the practical aspects of commitment and come back to our old friends, reward and recognition. Remember that you get the behaviour you reward and what gets measured gets done. However, this can be a little more complex in cross-functional teams . . .

A client in the telecommunications sector approached us for support on an internal project to integrate technical aspects of their offering; the project fell across a number of areas of responsibility and had been beset by problems at every stage. Here, it is sufficient to focus on one aspect of the problems, which was lack of buy-in to the project. The project was cross-functional with about 100 people on it, all of whom were working on it in addition to their primary line role. The project manager was concerned about lack of commitment to the project. One issue we became aware of was that the project had gone on so long that many of the team had received annual appraisals within the period in which they had been working on it. However, line managers had no real engagement with the project and so the work that individuals had done in support of the project was not included within the appraisals. My reaction was along the lines of: 'Duh'. Apart from the slightly shocking career management subtext to this story, it shouldn't really be any great surprise that there wasn't much commitment. If you're the boss and it's important to you and the organization, then make it important for other people too. Make it in their interests to commit.

A more positive commercial example is provided in Walter Isaacson's biography of Steve Jobs.[1] In spite of being a hugely successful global business, the world's largest by market capitalization at times, Apple both benefitted and suffered from Jobs' autonomy as CEO. While the company had a high-powered board of directors, and was subject to the same governance requirements as any publicly listed organization, it is quite clear that Jobs' unique position, experience and credibility as Apple's founder, bestowed on him autonomy almost unheard of in large public companies. Jobs maintained a laser-like focus on the common purpose and highest priorities. If the aim was to launch the iPad on a certain date, then he didn't really care what division you were in, who you worked for, or what the internal process was. The only thing which mattered was a successful launch. The end did not get confused with the means. The purpose was clear and effort, reward and recognition were clearly aligned.

The Channel Tunnel – a case study

The Channel Tunnel (Chunnel), a 50km rail tunnel linking the United Kingdom and France, opened in 1994 and has been described as the eighth wonder of the world. At its lowest point, it is 75m below the surface and, at 37.9km, it has the longest undersea portion of any tunnel in the world. The engineering was, and remains, exceptional; the organizational process and alignment of interests in its construction, less so. When travelling at high speed from the centre of London to Paris in just a few hours, it is easy to forget now that the Chunnel project also became a major case study of how not to align cross-functional teams.[2]

The whole project suffered from the sort of adversarial relationships between promoters and contractors that have dogged construction for many years and which in some areas, continue to this day. The competitive tender process encourages bidders to make the lowest and most optimistic price estimates. When added to the requirement for innovation and still-to-be-proven technology, the bidding process was implicitly incentivizing a short-term behavior (bid aggressively low to win) misaligned with the long-term reality (we've never done this before and need to build in contingency). The primary focus on costs in public sector projects was famously captured by US astronaut John Glenn. When asked what it felt like sitting atop a rocket about to launch, he replied: 'I felt about as good as anybody would, sitting in a capsule on top of a rocket that were both built by the lowest bidder.' The irony of course is that the cost of overruns is always more expensive than building in flexibility at the outset. The Chunnel was a year late and, at £4.65bn, 80 per cent over budget.[3]

Objectives were not clear or defined at the outset, and so it would have been impossible for rewards to contractors to have been directly linked to long-term goals. In actual fact, the original consortium consisted of construction companies and bankers whose primary objective was to make money on the construction and not on the operation, in spite of the original commercial project having a fifty-five-year life cycle (you get what you reward).

There was a positive corollary though, when it came to London Heathrow's Terminal 5 (T5)[4]. In this case, the client, BAA (British Airports Authority), learnt from previous experience in the sector and created what was then a unique contract between itself and its delivery partners that articulated a different approach to transparency and collaboration in managing risk. The basic logic was 'we're all in this together'. The success of the T5 project in using a partnership model received a significant endorsement when a similar model was employed for the London 2012 Olympics, the United Kingdom's most prestigious major construction programme in recent years and an outstanding success. In contrast to the Chunnel, in both of these examples, there was clarity in *common* purpose, a commitment to a *common* goal and the client did not labour under the illusion that the building contractors carried the technical and financial risks. If it didn't work and/or overran, everybody lost.

Common approach

With everybody heading towards the same outcome, the next step is a common approach as to how we will get there. This theme runs right through from high-level strategy to the application of standard operating procedures at the tactical level. If the points of contact between different functions or teams are complicated by different processes, or use of different language and different systems, then every project becomes a unique exercise in coordination and planning. Every time key players or teams change, newcomers will need to be trained in the approach in use. Let me offer two examples to illustrate the power of a common approach.

The first is the use of Standard Operating Procedures (SOPs). Just about every air force squadron in the world will have SOPs. These define in some detail the 'how we do business', effectively the Management Operations System. Bear in mind that SOPs are not rules, for which compliance is mandatory, or checklists, which are used to bring predictability and high reliability to repeat tasks and/or safety-critical actions. SOPs are more the standardization of operational process based on hard-won experience of what works best.

Of course, the SOPs for fighter operations in Afghanistan are different to the SOPs for helicopter search and rescue in the United Kingdom. So we have levels or a hierarchy of SOPs. The highest level is the internationally agreed best practice that only covers procedures for different national forces working together. The next level is our national procedures that define how we will conduct our own operations within the agreed international framework. And finally, local procedures that define operations for different aircraft types in detail. The key point is that each level is consistent with the one above; it just defines the local application in more detail. Use of SOPs is never the only possible approach to a problem, but in the absence of any reason or brief to the contrary, they define default best practice. By consistent application of SOPs we dramatically simplify planning and execution of complex operations. We don't start every task with a blank sheet of paper and reinvent the wheel; the basics are already all tied down.

Consider the use of SOPs on fighter operations. Defensive operations are by their nature even more reactive than offensive operations. It's impossible to plan in detail in advance, since what is required defensively depends wholly on who and what attacks you and how. I remember one of the large-scale Cold War scenario exercises that we still used to carry out in the early 1990s. Together with four other crews, my navigator and I were held on readiness in the aircraft shelters. We didn't even know who was in the other aircraft, just callsigns that defined how many other aircraft the crew were qualified to lead. An 'A' could lead anything, a 'B' was a four-ship (aircraft) leader, a 'C' was a 'pairs' leader, and a 'D' was the coffee boy, or more accurately a wingman. Operational callsigns tend not to be quite as cool as 'Maverick' and 'Goose'.

After half an hour of waiting, two of us were launched – myself (a B at that time) and a D. We were launched to join a combat air patrol over the North Sea, defending a defined block of airspace with four other aircraft already 'on station', that had taken off from a different fighter base. So we became a six-aircraft formation whose crews had not even coordinated remotely in this case – straight in at the deep end. We needed to start conducting intercept operations immediately in cohesion with the other aircraft. Can you imagine how complex this is? Who is supposed to do what, when, how and why?

Fortunately, this tricky issue had been anticipated in our version of 'Fighter Operations for Dummies' otherwise known as SOPs. The basic process for how different numbers of aircraft should coordinate and the responsibilities for different roles based on seniority of callsign have all been defined in advance. There was an A callsign already on the patrol leading the other three aircraft, and he told me and my D wingman to become his secondary formation. Nothing else was required. Everybody knew what to do. We were able to operate six high-performance fighter aircraft on complex intercept operations in a highly reactive unpredictable environment simply by resorting to SOPs. No extra training, no plan, no brief.

SOPs make otherwise complex tasks predictable (which also implies safer). That in turn improves flexibility. We can change team members or whole teams within the bigger mission on a daily or even hourly basis without any loss of capability and with no training burden. To see a direct example of the benefit in efficiency and effectiveness, consider the use of standard processes on the Red Arrows.

In short, the Red Arrows have nine red jets with a red, white and blue smoke system and they have the not unpleasant role of showing off for a living! That's the basic job specification. In practice, the flying display is divided into two halves. In the first half, all nine jets are together following the leader in different shapes. This is difficult to do with perfect symmetry, but fairly simple in concept. In the second half of the display, the formation splits into three elements. It is not possible in these few pages to describe the relative complexity in safely coordinating the three elements, in shows with vastly differing terrain and weather, in order to always have something happening in front of the crowd with no timing errors or gaps.

An example second-half manoeuvre involves seven aircraft pulling up into a loop in formation. On the way down, the pilots all rotate away from each other and continue down towards the ground. If each aircraft is travelling at about 400 mph (640 kph), they are opening away from each other, with a huge horizontal footprint, at about 800 mph (1280 kph). Imagine doing that manouevre, vertically downwards, into a valley with 6,000 ft (2,000m) sides. Because that is what the team had to do in Buochs in Switzerland (check it out on Google Earth).

This was clearly going to pose some problems. And this was a big show. The French display team, the Patrouille de France, was there. One hundred thousand people at a seaside show would be regarded as a pretty standard show; however, the presence of the professional peer group in the form of eight French display pilots immediately made this a big show! In spite of my banter, the French team is extremely good, very professional and does a show which is broadly similar in concept to the Red Arrows in two halves, the second half containing the dynamic manoeuvring. For the show at Buochs, the Patrouille had rehearsed onsite the day before, on the Friday before the weekend airshow, and concluded that it would not be possible to fly a second half inside the valley; this would be a first half show only. The Red Arrows were not due to arrive at Buochs until the Saturday and in fact, one of the aircraft had a problem en route and the whole formation ended up diverting to another airfield in Switzerland, Emmen. The engineers managed to fix the broken aircraft and a decision was made to leave them at Emmen. The pilots took off from Emmen and flew straight into the display at Buochs, not having rehearsed and never having been to Buochs before. And the team flew the whole show, first and second half, after which the Patrouille may have grudgingly admitted to being a tiny bit impressed.

The key to that success lay in the different modus operandi of the teams. The French team normally used to rehearse onsite. This has some obvious performance and safety benefits. The unique challenges posed by each display site are identified and dealt with in advance. The Red Arrows had a more systematic approach to display planning. The airborne shapes can be projected onto the ground and the team uses a standard template of critical points in the ground pattern to overlay on a map of the display site. This is then compared to a satellite photograph of the display site to identify what the key features shown on the map will actually look like. For the Buochs show, this method was taken a step further and map of Buochs was overlaid on a map of the team's home base in Lincolnshire (possibly the flattest place in the United Kingdom!) to understand what the display would look like at home base with 6,000-foot hills on either side. And the team went and flew the show as if it was in Switzerland. The Leader even flew with 2 per cent less power to simulate the altitude. And it didn't quite work. So they did it again. And by the time they arrived at Buochs, they had worked out how to fly the show in that valley.

You might argue that that is an enormous effort to achieve quality at the expense of quantity. This appears to be the case, but, in practice, the opposite is generally true. It takes a long time to systemize and optimize your planning process to the required level of detail. However, once you get it right, you reap the benefits. Without any need to rehearse onsite, the team did two more displays en route to Switzerland on the Friday. And bear in mind that these plans can be produced in about 30 minutes. And any one of the three pilots on the team who looked after navigation could produce a similar-looking plan to a similar standard.

What we are trying to do with a common approach is not to impose some 'Big Brother' mindless systemized approach. We are actually building a common chassis onto which we layer those aspects of a problem that are unique or peculiar to the operating environment. But we are all using the same chassis to work from. We don't have people going off in random directions doing work that is uncoordinated with the rest of the team, or cannot be easily integrated due to using non-standard processes or hardware. People have thrown this back at me as being all very well for the military, but not as easy for the agile, flexible 'real world'. My response is that we take off at night in bad weather and people shoot at us. We are quite agile. A common approach is not what makes us inflexible; it's what makes us flexible.

If rules and regulation are the hard boundaries of 'the space' we get to operate in, SOPs define an inner boundary of agreed and systemized best practice. SOPs do not have to be followed blindly and deviation is permitted if a situation demands it, but you need a good reason to go down that route.

Communication

The final leg of the alignment tripod is communication. And in this case, I don't mean communication as a behaviour. I mean communication as a process. How do we get the right information to the right people at the right time? How do we communicate with clarity? Our experience of commercial clients is that organizations spend a lot of time and effort on communication skills, but almost exclusively focus on behaviour. They might train using Myers Briggs tools, or developing coaching skills or working on giving and receiving feedback. These things can all be very powerful, especially if they are new to the trainees and are well delivered. However, very few people train in communication as a process. How do I analyse a complex problem, come up with a cogent solution and articulate it clearly? How do I cascade information throughout an organization without losing clarity or engagement? How do we keep people updated on what is relevant to them without simply engaging in communication overload? How do we manage knowledge and information across the organization?

The military tend to almost have the opposite problem, investing considerable time and effort in training in communication as a process and concentrating less on the behavioural aspects. Back on our fighter mission, the AWACS is effectively the communication node. When I am flying along in my jet, I fly with two (or more) radios on. One in my left ear is set to a high volume and is the means by which I communicate locally with my team. We are constantly sharing information that is only really relevant to us locally. However, every now and again something happens locally which people in the wider mission might need to know, or at least benefit from knowing. Hence, in my right ear is another radio on a lower volume which is tuned to the AWACS. When something happens locally that other people need to know, I pass it to the AWACS and the crew passes it on to the *relevant* parties. Note that the AWACS acts as a filter here. Not all information goes to everybody. The aim is to get the right information to the right people at the right time. And sometimes the AWACS crew will become aware of things that we should know locally, and pass that information on.

To make this happen, we set up a communication plan, which is exactly what it says on the tin. We plan the lines of communication in advance.

Who will need access to what sources of information? How will they get it, whether actively or passively? This might be as simple as just setting up weekly or monthly open forum meetings – not complicated. But you know how difficult the reality can be. Big organizations are political and hierarchical, not necessarily well structured for the project or problem in hand, and lines of communication can be always open (email overload), always closed (brick wall of silence) or non-existent (do your own thing and hope for the best).

Right information, right people, right time . . .

Empowerment

Having built and structured a team or organization which is all pointing in the same direction, it is now time to empower. The general in the headquarters in Qatar can't possibly be making tactical decisions for the solider on the street corner in Kabul. And the great thing about empowerment is that 'when you buy one, you get one free'. Empowerment drives agility and performance, however ownership of the plan and the execution is also a very powerful motivator. Commitment is essential, however, once you add ownership, you then get engagement – a kind of 'commitment plus'. You have 'skin in the game' in terms of what the outcome looks like.

Very recently I ran a communication and alignment programme for a small engineering company undergoing a transformational change from contract manufacturing to aerospace technology. Having given the senior business unit leaders the strategic priorities for the business, the MD asked those leaders what their own missions should be, how they would measure success and what tasks they implicitly needed to complete. At the end of the day, the MD commented that one of the biggest benefits, which he had failed to anticipate, was that people now had 'skin in the game'. They had defined their own direction and priorities and were implicitly incentivized to deliver against their own words.

My experience when talking to people about empowerment and particularly in the context of my military background, is that they tend to have preconceptions about the military, which often include words such as 'command' and 'control'. There are two issues with this type of preconception. First, those words tend to mean something different in military parlance. 'Command', in particular, does not imply micromanagement or orders. It is about accepting responsibility for the deployment of people and resources plus setting and communicating direction. None of those sound like such a bad thing for any organization. It also implies clearly defined accountability, something which can be lacking when the matrix structure provides a convenient excuse for nobody to be really directly accountable for anything. The second issue is that military leaders were some of the first proponents of empowerment. Nelson and Von Moltke were giving their subordinates wide freedom of manoeuvre hundreds of years before management thinking and business schools caught up.

Empowerment in the modern military is captured in something called 'Mission Command'. It is not now and never has been uniformly embedded and deployed. However, in certain parts of the military, in particular special forces and fast-jet operations, empowerment is really the only option available. It is simply not possible for one person to micromanage the complexity of a big fast-moving mission. To try to do so will result in decision-making bottlenecks, destroy agility and result in almost certain failure.

So mission commanders are told what is to be achieved, why and when by, but given ownership and freedom as to how to achieve it. The same thing happens within a big mission itself. The commander will agree the role of the different elements with element leaders and ensure coordination. However, decision-making responsibility is delegated to the lowest practical level.

With a clear understanding of common purpose and higher intentions, and the broad roles of everyone else in achieving that purpose, a common approach and the means of sharing new information, individuals and teams can be set free to own local problems and solve them as they see fit. Actually, when you think about it, there is really no other way of doing it, unless you want to read about your organization portrayed as silo'd and disconnected in a book ... which brings me nicely back to my former bank. It seems a little harsh to throw spears without commenting on potential solutions. What would I do?

Well, it's not difficult to know what a customer-centric solution would look like: an internal system whereby a customer's records are stored in one central location that can be accessed by one person for all routine service enquiries. More than that, though, is the need for a mindset and structural change. I want the person I deal with to act as a single point of contact and take ownership of my problems. This simple idea probably requires wide structural changes and a level of empowerment that is currently absent. Unfortunately, I don't see those things changing unless the bank appoints a very senior executive, who is personally obsessive about the service experience, is clever enough to simplify complexity, and has a mandate and authority to make the sweeping changes that are necessary to organizational structure.

This is where the Steve Jobs approach works well. Among his many strengths and weaknesses, what comes through loud and clear in Isaacson's biography is Jobs' passion for his core business and what it stands for, an obsession for great products and a relentless focus on simplification. And he had the mandate and decision-making authority to cut through the noise of conflicting priorities and make outcomes happen, without worrying about local Key Performance Indicators (KPIs) and departmental infighting. How many other senior executives are truly passionate about their core business, are obsessive (and objective!) about the customer experience, and are relentlessly focused on making that service experience seamless? If my former bank thought like that, they clearly wouldn't have designed the organization they did.

Summary of key points

- Design of cross-functional teams needs to be constantly benchmarked against what you are trying to achieve:
  - Design shouldn't be driven only by internal structure or process
  - Think *effects*; put together the team you need, not the team you have
  - The task leader should be the best person to lead the task irrespective of seniority
  - Everyone else needs to let them lead

- Building the capability for high performance:
  - Clarity in common purpose – everyone pointing at the same *collective* goal
  - Alignment
    - Commitment through clear purpose, reinforcing behaviours, and reward and recognition
    - Common approach – define and use standard default best practices; don't re-invent the wheel; free up your brainpower for the clever stuff
    - Communication (process) – right information, right people, right time
  - Empowerment
    - Facilitates agility and flexibility in achieving outcomes
    - Also involves and engages people through owning their own part of the mission

Getting stuff done

Chapter 5

From desire to outcome (Delivery)

We have the right people: team players with the right competencies. And we have aligned their efforts in ways in which they have absolutely clarity in what they are trying to achieve and why. And having defined that for themselves, they are emotionally invested with 'skin in the game'. However, the only relevant measure of ultimate success is the ability to close the gap between vision and reality, or between desire and outcome.

This chapter drills down into the tactical elements of delivery and the ability to get stuff done. It comprises three sections that could be chapters in their own right but, due to their synergy and causality, are presented as three sub-sections of the same issue (delivery): planning, communication (of the plan) and execution. The second chapter in this section, on learning, closes the gap between what got talked about and what got done.

Plans and planning

Planning is an unnatural process. It is far more fun to do something. The nicest thing about not planning is that failure comes as a surprise and is not preceded by worry or tension.

Sir John Harvey-Jones

Planning for success

It doesn't matter whether you are responsible for the Chunnel or a display on the Red Arrows, if you fail to plan effectively, then you have relinquished ownership and control of what you end up delivering. In hindsight, almost every aspect of the Chunnel project was set up for failure. The scope was not clearly defined at the outset. Analysis of the issues was severely time constrained by the bidding process. Commercial forecasts were not objectively stress-tested; in practice, the cross-Channel ferry companies did not just stand by and watch their livelihood disappear while the appearance of budget airlines fundamentally changed the competitive environment. The fixed-price bidding process meant that there were no contingency plans or resources. Eurotunnel, the operating company, was in huge debt on completion of the tunnel and was forced into bankruptcy measures by a French court in 2006 (financial restructuring meant that it did continue to trade). It's now a case study in how not to plan or deliver a major project.

I've never seen a Red Arrows display that wasn't planned in detail in advance, but I have seen lots of examples in aviation of where incorrect or incomplete plans have been the precursor to poor performance or worse. One of my most embarrassing moments was taking off with insufficient fuel for a transit flight across Canada in a Tornado aircraft in bad weather. That might sound like a ridiculous scenario: How could you do something that stupid? It was actually quite a routine flight though. I did the fuel plan on a scrap of paper while dealing with lots of distractions and made a mistake. Almost as bad, I was experienced and nobody else in the formation did their own checks or challenged me. The outcome was no worse than some red faces when we returned to our start point an hour after take-off, but it could have been a lot more serious.

I have been more routinely guilty of incomplete planning in my business. Why would that be? Planning is in my DNA. I know how to do it. I understand the value. The problem is that not only is planning not as much fun as delivery, it's a cost centre. When I have finite resources available and competing priorities, then I prioritize delivery. I know it's a short-term decision that will have long-term consequences, but I still sometimes fail to allocate enough resource to planning. I always regret it when it happens. To fail to plan is to plan to fail.

Plans and planning

In preparing for battle I have always found that plans are useless but planning is indispensable.

Dwight D. Eisenhower

Given that no less a figure from military history as Eisenhower thinks that plans are useless, are we on the right track? The problem is that the effect of *friction* (Chapter 1) means that the plan rarely, if ever, works exactly as envisaged. So why bother? Well, when it comes to long-term issues, the answer is probably: don't. You would be better off with a clear 'intent' aligned with the strategy, and to make detailed plans only for shorter time horizons that can be foreseen with some degree of confidence.

At some point though, the intent needs to be broken down into tangible bite-sized chunks and people need to do things. For many environments, including fast-jet aviation, even at the tactical level, friction will wreak havoc with plans. However, the paradox is that even though 'no plan survives first contact with the enemy', the planning process is not wasted effort. The important bit is not so much the piece of paper or the presentation that is produced, or 'the plan', but the brainpower, time and effort that was expended in analysing the problem and scenario modelling the options and contingencies. These are what help us navigate through the fog of execution. Plans are useless, but planning is indispensable . . .

Even the plan itself does serve some useful purposes though, with all due respect to General Eisenhower, who was almost certainly just proving a point. It gives us a start point for the organization and allocation of our resources, as well as stress testing that resources are sufficient. 'Big hairy audacious goals' can be inspiring and motivating, but it is helpful to play within the realms of the humanly possible. The plan gives visibility to all players about higher level intent, why they are doing what they are doing and how it all ties together. Implicit within this are the organization and coordination of different elements – the articulation of the common approach towards the objective.

As a leader you may wish to empower people and teams to solve their local problems as they see fit, but there are probably limits as to what is permissible without reference back to higher authority, perhaps due to finite resources or the impact on other players; these freedoms and constraints are identified within the plan. Finally, the plan provides a benchmark against which to measure progress. If the execution fails to meet the milestones in the plan, that is a pretty strong indicator of problems ahead. So the greater value is in planning rather than in the plan itself, however a strong plan is still an essential precursor to successful execution.

The right solution to the wrong problem

If I had only one hour to save the world, I would spend 55 minutes defining the problem, and only five minutes finding the solution.
                                        Attributed to Albert Einstein

Just because we have the best hammer does not mean that every problem is a nail.
                              Barack Obama (Speech at West Point, 2014)

Before diving into the mechanics of how to plan for decisive success, it is worth considering some of the challenges ahead. One scenario that I have seen a lot is providing the right solution to the wrong problem. General Stanley McChrystal offers an interesting perspective on this issue in *Team of Teams*,[1] where he discusses the difference (in his world) between efficiency and effectiveness. He was in command of possibly the best resourced and trained military fighting machine in history but was, by many measures, losing the battle against insurgents in Iraq. McChrystal describes his forces as incredibly efficient but often ineffective. They were efficient in things that were irrelevant for the problem they faced and the plans predicated on leveraging their efficiency were fundamentally flawed from the outset. The issue McChrystal faced was one of asymmetric warfare where it was not enough to be more capable (in the efficient sense) than the bad guys, because they were actually playing a wholly different 'game' by a different set of rules; the efficiency was irrelevant. Examples of this issue abound in both military history and the wider world. Consider this apocryphal quote from the end of the Vietnam war:

> **American Colonel to his Vietnamese counterpart:** 'You know you never defeated us in a major battle.'
> **Vietnamese Colonel:** 'That may be true but it is also irrelevant.'

In the commercial world, the plans of the legacy large (often national) airlines to differentiate on quality were largely made irrelevant when deregulation allowed the low-cost carriers to compete instead on price. Technology has fundamentally disrupted many industries, lowering barriers to entry, reducing the defensibility (or relevance) of intellectual property and completely changing the rules of the game, sometimes in astonishingly short periods. As I write, Uber is currently smashing through local cartels and protectionist groups that have kept taxi fares up, all over the world. Kodak was founded in 1892 and for much of the twentieth century was the dominant global player in manufacture of photographic film. However, in a period of only around ten years at the start of the twenty-first century, Kodak went from that dominant position to filing for 'Chapter 11' bankruptcy protection in the United States. As with the colonel in Vietnam, McChrystal in Iraq and taxi companies the world over, Kodak had framed the wrong problem and was making plans based on assumptions that were simply untrue.

I saw a variation on this issue recently in the airline industry. One of the measures against which airlines are assessed is their 'on time performance' (OTP). This is essentially a measure of punctuality versus the schedule. While this sounds like a relevant performance indicator, even this simple definition is fraught with imprecision. Improving OTP can either be a planning (scheduling) or an execution issue, and comparisons are highly sensitive to the type of aircraft flown on what route (busyness of airspace and airports).

The aspect on which I was approached to consult was well defined though: turnaround time, that is, the time from an aircraft arriving at the gate to departing again. The prospective client was the airport operator, who wanted airlines to perform better against planned turnaround times. In its opinion, the problem lay with service companies (the suppliers employed by airlines who provide the servicing of the aircraft on the ground), and in particular their resourcing. However, the service companies are just one part of a much more complex system with all sorts of interdependencies. It seemed to me that there was a distinct risk that they were trying to provide an efficiency solution to an effectiveness problem. The dialogue is ongoing . . .

As you can see, we almost can't put too much effort into framing the issue of what and why before diving into how, but at some point, the focus has turn to the details – how are we actually going to make this happen?

The mission planning process

The fine detail of how we plan a military fighter mission may not be relevant to many readers, and I don't pretend to offer a solution that would have transformed Eurotunnel, but I think that you will find that the underlying principles translate well to most environments. The process can be summarized in five simple stages:

Aim
Start at the end
Analysis
Tactics
Contingencies

Aim

The aim is a concise statement of what it is we are trying to achieve – an articulation of what success looks like. It is difficult to think of better criteria than the common SMART mnemonic as a means of defining a good aim. The aim should be:

S pecific
M easurable
A chievable
R elevant
T ime-bounded

The SMART criteria are largely self-explanatory. It will be difficult to know if you have ever achieved success unless the aim is specific and measurable; the resources must be sufficient to make the mission at least theoretically possible; the mission should align with higher intent; and being time-bounded is an important sub-criterion of being measurable – if the plan is open-ended, how will we ever know if are successful; it should at least be possible to identify milestones or indicators of progress.

It may help to provide context by reference to an example mission. It was a training sortie that I flew from Scotland: eight Tornados versus eight Dutch F16 fighters. The aim was to prevent any Dutch fighters crossing a line in the North Sea (simulated border of a country) between 19.00 and 20.00. Success was absolutely clearly defined. If no Dutch jet crossed the line before 20.00, then the mission would be achieved. If one crossed the line, then it would not. This mission was clearly specific, measurable and time-bounded. You will have to take my word that it was achievable with the resources allocated (note that 'achievable' is a slightly less specific criterion than the first two; inspirational leadership has overcome many practical problems and apparently insurmountable barriers. However, one has to believe that one's mission is theoretically possible). Relevance might prove more challenging. One would like to think that when you were given your mission, the wider context of why it is relevant was explained. If the Dutch jet is shot down (simulated in this case!) just after crossing the border, is that still a mission success? Well, strictly speaking, as defined earlier, the answer is no. One assumes that there is a good reason why the mission was defined exactly like that. Perhaps even crossing the border is a moral victory or demonstration of weakness that might be exploited in the future.

This illustrates an important point though, that the aim needs to be thought through in some detail to ensure that it is the correct one. Aims and objectives are not often passed down with the clarity described earlier. In that case, teams will need to take it upon themselves to make sure that they really understand what they are being asked to try and achieve and why. Note that 'what' and 'why' are highly interdependent. Having worked out 'what', it may become apparent on trying to unravel 'why' that is important, that we have in fact, incorrectly identified the 'what.' The 'what' is the task, while the 'why' is the relevance to higher level intent. Or, to put it another way, the 'what' is the mission, and the 'why' is the vision, the reason that the mission is worth doing. If the task is not clearly aligned with higher level intent, then it is probably not the right task.

Your aim might be a successful product launch, a financial target, a market penetration target or perhaps a customer satisfaction metric. If your division is purely a cost centre, or 'business as usual' does not lend itself to SMART aims, then it is worth trying to artificially contrive some. Remember that humans generally respond well to purpose,[2] and how will you know if you have achieved anything, if you didn't set out to? As you will see when we come on to debriefing, it's difficult to learn from an experience that didn't have an aim or a plan to start off with.

Objectives might be regarded as subsidiary aims. They may be critical enablers or constraints, but they are not ends in their own right. An example objective for a military pilot might be flight safety, or more specifically, no flight safety mishaps. That is clearly desirable but is not the aim of the mission. Many times I have heard executives in 'high-risk' industries say that 'our number one aim is safety'. This surely fails the common sense test; if that is true, stay in bed. The aim is to deliver the desired outcome. Safety is the most important constraint as to how it must be achieved. Flight safety is not an end in its own right. If we weren't trying to use aircraft in complicated operations to achieve some effect, then we wouldn't even be discussing safety. Don't confuse the aim and objectives. The aim is what it is; the objectives are normally enablers or constraints.

Start at the end

Military pilots need to have a proactive rather than a reactive approach to planning and execution. Having got clarity in the task, they work backwards from the end point to where they are now, to see what needs to be done between now and the end, and how much time can be allocated to each phase.

On my training mission back over the North Sea, we had to defend the line between 19.00 and 20.00, so the first thing I do is work out my timeline:

19.00 On task
18.30 Rendezvous refueller (air-to-air refuelling aircraft)
18.00 Take off
17.45 Check in
17.30 Walk for aircraft
16.30 Sortie brief
16.00 Finish planning
14.00 All crews available
13.30 Lead crews brainstorm

This is a very tactical level example; however, I am sure that you can see that the same principle applies to larger scale tasks and longer timelines.

For reasons that are not immediately obviously connected to flying jets or management consultancy, I was a co-founder and part-owner of a lingerie retail outlet. When we found the premises, we asked some builders to come and quote to fit the shop out. At this stage, their approach was purely reactive. They looked at what they thought was required, worked out how long it would take and how much it would cost. I was completely fine with that; it couldn't really be any other way. We agreed on a completion date, I built in one week of flexibility and we started to publicize an opening party for four weeks later. After two weeks, it was obvious to me that the work would not be completed on time and I spoke to the builders. Their mindset was simply that it might take a bit longer. The problem for me was that having been awarded the work, they stayed in *reactive* mode; there was no *proactive* ownership of the outcome, which included the agreed target date, or tracking of progress. We just about achieved the party date, although not without some very late nights in the run-up doing the final painting myself! Start with the end in mind . . .

Analysis

The same kind of flow as with Bruce Tuckman's 'forming, norming, storming, performing' model[3] for new teams happens, even for existing teams or experienced team players, when faced with a new problem, task or project requiring a plan. There is an analysis phase of just individually and collectively getting your heads around the issue and framing it, followed by an action phase where you refine and evaluate options, and develop a specific course of action. This is a very common concept. How could it be any other way?

In *The McKinsey Mind*, Ethan Rasiel[4] describes the initial brainstorm that takes place at the start of a new client engagement. Rasiel talks about a hypothesis-based approach where the team shares every piece of information known to them about a problem and then, rather than trying to come up with an intellectually rigorous solution based on some sort of inductive or deductive logic (potentially a pointless pursuit where any one of a number of approaches might be workable), the team jumps straight to its best guess answer. It then works out what would need to be true or untrue for the hypothesis to be true and thereby prove or disprove it, while simultaneously evolving the hypothesis through each iteration as new data comes to light. IDEO, the Californian design consultancy, undertakes a process that starts similarly in concept at the initiation of a new design engagement.[5] The aim in both cases is to attack the problem from lots of angles simultaneously, get as much data and as many ideas as possible on the table, and start to form an initial hypothesis about the likely most productive lines of attack on the problem.

In the competitive environment of military aviation, we use a simple outcome-driven method to analyse the problem. In many ways, it is just a variation of a SWOT (Strengths, Weaknesses, Opportunities, Threats) analysis. The difference is that the variation I describe here is not just a piece of analysis to lay out the issues; it also includes synthesis to lead us to an outcome. Threats and weaknesses are rolled into one – combined, these are all barriers to success. Analysis of strengths now naturally leads us to opportunities where competitive advantage exists; those define our plan.

Threats

Threats are those things which, quite simply, will stop you achieving your goals. They fall into three broad categories.

External threats

I cannot know too much about my adversary. I want to know how fast their aircraft go, how fast and far their missiles go, how much they get paid, if their family receives a pension if they get shot down – anything that might influence their ability and motivation to compete or fight.

The primary source of this information is our intelligence database. We have a whole group of people, even within the Air Force (not to mention all the other national intelligence assets and agencies), whose full-time job is 'intelligence', to be the subject matter experts and knowledge champions on intelligence-related matters. Intelligence capture can be either active or passive.

Active capture might include simply using a competitor's products or services. The US military has a long history of covert (and sometimes overt) acquisition of the systems of potentially hostile nations, in the first instance to analyse the capability, and then to actually use those systems to train against. Ethics and good business practice might be slightly more restraining on the commercial potential for active capture, however when you are talking about a competitor whose products are available in a commercial marketplace, then why not simply buy them?

Another source of active capture is information provided by new joiners from competitors. Confidentiality restrictions and good practice determine what is and isn't appropriate for the joiner to share, but there is a mine of intelligence simply sitting inside the heads of your people, if only you asked them.

Passive capture relates to the mine of information that crosses your radar every day, if you have a process to record it and then leverage it. We will look at knowledge management in Chapter 6.

Environmental threats

Environmental threats are the external threats that affect everybody equally. So, on my training mission in Scotland, it was night-time and it was dark. These issues place some limits on our tactics as to what is possible. Simultaneously, however, they may offer opportunities to use tactics that would not have been possible by day. Your environmental threats might be macroeconomic (e.g. reduced retail spending), customer-led (e.g. change in procurement policy by a significant public sector customer) or perhaps the threat of a change in regulation (e.g. increased capital holding requirements for banks). Whatever the issue, the first priority is a requirement to cope with the constraint and the second is to see how the constraint might be turned to an advantage.

Internal threats (weaknesses)

Internal threats are those barriers to success that exist within your own team and organization. For me, when I was on a squadron, one obvious internal threat was that we were always resource-limited. Contrary to some perceptions about the military, we were always over-tasked and under-resourced. On my training mission, there may not have been a spare aircraft. If one broke, we were down to seven. Your internal threats could be issues like morale, skill base, training, resources and so on. This might be a slightly more difficult conversation than analysing the external threats – nobody likes admitting to weakness. However, the internal threats will do you down at least as much as anything the competition might throw at you. You may as well be honest with yourself and plan around them.

Strengths

If analysis of the threats or barriers to success involves some soul-searching and has a slightly negative (I prefer 'realistic') feel about it, then analysis of strengths is an excuse for some chest-thumping. What are we good at? What skills, resources and capabilities can we employ to our advantage? My Tornado jet was very fast: Can we use that to tactical advantage? It is a two-crew aircraft. There are some pros and cons to that. The dynamic between the two individuals is extremely subtle; however, if you can get that right, there is a potential synergy there. With the right division of responsibilities and clear communication, two brains should be able to unravel a complex situation more effectively and quickly than one.

And we are subject matter experts. We really know our own products. If you ever visit a fighter squadron, you will always find somebody with their head buried deep in the red Top Secret files with all the detailed technical specifications for our own systems. We understand the strengths and weaknesses of our own assets to a highly advanced level of technical detail, which allows us to employ them to play to our *relative* strengths. For instance, most radars will give better performance when looking up into clear skies than when trying to find a target moving at low level overland against the clutter of terrain and background noise. However, this needs to be offset against the relative performance advantages and disadvantages of operating at high or low level, including increased fuel burn, and also missile performance – which generally is much better at a high level. Optimizing your tactics clearly demands a detailed knowledge of both your own systems and what you are up against.

Tactics (where is the best opportunity for success?)

At some point, the time for analysis will be over, and it will be time to commit to action. This is the core of the planning process. *Who* will do *what, when, why and how*? We already have *task clarity*, so now it is time to get clarity on the other key drivers of team effectiveness:

- Role clarity
- Allocation of resources – time, people, assets

It is worth noting that time is the only resource that is always finite and cannot be scaled. If the task is time sensitive, or involves conflicting priorities in the simultaneous deployment of resources, then establishing those priorities, and managing the timeline, will be critical from the outset.

In the same way that your strategy should identify where your organization can have competitive advantage, the aim of our process thus far is to identify the best opportunity for success. Our tactics should play to our relative strengths and, wherever possible, avoid playing on a level or disadvantaged playing surface. We aim to take the battle to the opposition at a time and place of our choosing.

You will notice on the news that many military operations are conducted at night. Why would we do that? We are sociable people; we like to have a beer in the evening. Well, the primary reason is that we generally possess a technology and skill advantage at night which is significantly reduced by day. Why would we do battle on equal terms, when we can choose to massively stack the odds in our favour?

Smart individuals, teams and organizations never choose to play on equal terms. Large construction groups do not bid for small projects, no matter what the margins, where their scale bestows no advantage to them in the bidding process. Budget airlines do not compete on quality. Clever salespeople do not pretend to compete against their adversary's greatest strength; they make it irrelevant. The aim is always to work smarter, not harder.

Contingencies

> If I appear always prepared, it is because before entering on an undertaking I have meditated for long and have foreseen what may occur. **It is not genius** which reveals to me suddenly and secretly what I should do in circumstances unexpected by others; it is thought and meditation.
>
> Napoleon (emphasis introduced)

The real key to long-term success though, is to prepare for the unexpected. The military is at heart a Plan B organization, or even Plan C or D. We are always thinking 'what if'; what could go wrong here? And I am not just talking about disaster recovery – the big red book of emergency processes that sits gathering dust until the disaster happens. I am talking about a cultural approach to the everyday stuff. The more variables and risk involved, and the less time to stop and analyse in the heat of the moment, then the more effort is expended in contingency planning.

By way of example, I come back to the Red Arrows. Every morning we used to have a weather briefing, where the whole team would meet together at the start of the day. For 2 minutes at the end, every day, we would discuss an aircraft technical issue – how you would deal with a technical problem in the air. It's as if we did 2 minutes of professional development every day. Over the weeks and months you cover an awful lot of material that might otherwise have been forgotten, before you need the knowledge at the critical moment.

Every time we flew, we would have a sortie brief. For 2 minutes at the end, we would cover a major emergency during the show – something that could be relevant to the operating base or display site or weather conditions on the day. How would we get an aircraft out of the show if we had to? What would we do with that aircraft? What would we do with the other aircraft? How would we change the shapes and smokes so that we still had symmetry for the rest of the show?

Now of course we were just talking about random hypothetical events, but over time you work through a lot of scenarios. We were not trying to reduce every problem to an exercise in process or compliance, but to instil a way of thinking about things, the underlying principles behind the decision-making and where the priorities lie – this can be far more valuable than the specifics. What happens over time is that you build a mental database of things that might go wrong and how to deal with them, and when things do go wrong, you dip into the database. The thing that goes wrong is never exactly the same as the scenario discussed, but it is likely that we covered something similar, or with the same underlying priorities, at some point. And so what we do is to dip into the database and shape whatever is there to fit the actual situation we are facing. The decision that we made over a coffee in the crewroom with our feet on the table is always going to be better than the decision you make under enormous personal stress in the heat of the moment. What we do in practice is to make the high-pressure decisions in low-pressure environments. When the pressure's on, we do what we planned to do.

Upside down at 400mph: What's the plan?

The return on the investment in planning only becomes clear during execution, in particular if things start going wrong. Let me give you an example. One winter during my time in the Red Arrows, we did some training in Moron in Spain. Our own planning was clearly slightly deficient on this occasion since it turned out that at that time of year,

Moron tended to have a significant problem with birds flying in the vicinity of the airfield. And these were not little British sparrows, more like some southern European juggernaut of the skies. Not surprisingly, when we were operating nine jets very close to the ground three times a day, some of the birds took umbrage with the imposition on their playground and decided to fight back.

My personal experience of this problem occurred while inverted about 300ft (100m) above the ground, rolling around the smoke of two other jets, while a third jet rolled the opposite way around the smoke in front of me. At that moment, a rather large bird bid goodbye to life while puncturing a hole in my wing at 400mph (640kph). The manoeuvre was called the 'Corkscrew' and involved Red 6 flying inverted along the display line (in this case the runway). Red 7 would fly in formation directly underneath, looking straight up into his cockpit – I guess it was like Top Gun after all. Red 8 started around 30m behind Reds 6 and 7 on the left of their smoke, and I (Red 9) started a further 30m behind on the right. On a call from Red 6, Red 8 would start rotating around the smoke in an anticlockwise direction, and I would rotate clockwise. We would pass each other in opposite directions at the top and bottom of our rotations, hopefully maintaining a similar distance apart! The manoeuvre is shown graphically in Figure 5.1.

Suffice to say that the dynamics of this manoeuvre mean that there are quite a few variables at play; if it looked complicated from the ground, it definitely concentrated the mind in the air. While passing through

Figure 5.1 The corkscrew

the inverted position towards the end of the last rotation, I felt and heard a thump and immediately assumed a birdstrike. This was not really the time for extended analysis of the problem. Nor was there a checklist or SOP for what to do when having a birdstrike while inverted very close to three other aircraft, not to mention the ground. However, we had spoken about these sorts of issues on many occasions. The first priority was to clear the formation – relatively straightforward in this case – and I just rolled out the right way up and broke off the back of the formation. There was no crowd to worry about on this occasion (training sortie), so I could start to think about my own jet.

While there are some guiding principles and procedures for birdstrikes, common sense also applies. In the ideal world, you want to do a low-speed handling check at height to see how the aircraft performs at lower speeds and when you put the landing gear and the flaps down, in case there is damage to the control surfaces or services. However, the counter argument is that you might be leaking fuel or hydraulic oil from a hole, and your situation is about to get a whole lot worse – it had felt like a big thump, so you want to land as quickly as possible. Added to these factors, there is the minor issue of the rest of the formation.

As I had rolled out, the manoeuvre ended anyway, signified by Red 6 calling 'smoke off, go'. This is also the cue for Reds 1 to 5 to commence their next manoeuvre from the opposite end of the runway. The significance of this is that, for safety reasons, only the element doing a manoeuvre in front of the crowd is allowed to use the radio. This is part of a wider policy about how the radio is used as a safety break. Anytime anything out of sequence happens on the radio, then the whole show stops. So I had a birdstrike that sounded serious and had caused unknown damage. I had broken away from my element (Reds 6, 7 and 8), and was climbing in a teardrop pattern to do a quick slow-speed handling check as I reversed direction to land straight back on to the runway, as shown in Figure 5.2. However, there were five jets coming down the line of the runway towards me at 300ft (100m) doing low-level aerobatic manoeuvres and I was not supposed to speak on the radio to warn them of my predicament.

This is where one sees the value of contingency planning as a way of thinking more than simply an exercise in process or compliance.

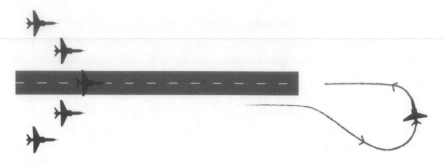

Figure 5.2 The emergency situation

It defies credibility that we would have considered exactly this scenario in advance. However, we had discussed variations on the theme, where one pilot has a critical problem while the other element is using the radio. Having practised the show many times, I knew exactly the sequence of radio transmissions from the other element. So while reversing direction to land and slowing down to check the handling, I waited for a known gap in the radio sequence, and called '9's out with a birdstrike'. This immediately implies to the Team Leader that he should stop the manoeuvre and he calls 'flying it through'. Nobody else will now speak or do anything until told to, other than one pilot (pre-nominated) immediately requesting landing clearance for me from Air Traffic Control on a different frequency, and warning them that I have a problem so that emergency services will be ready. Now that the radio sequence had stopped, I informed the leader that I was reversing direction in order to land and he led his section away from the runway and my direction of turn.

The subsequent landing was uneventful although the aircraft did have a decent sized hole in the wing. Fortunately, the internal fuel tank had not been punctured. There is never a specific contingency plan for a one-off unique combination of unusual circumstances, but it's a bit like the difference between the plan and planning. In this case, it was contingency *planning* that added the value, rather any defined plan. It was the time, effort and brainpower that we had invested in talking about all sorts of related scenarios that allow you to come up with something viable in the heat of the moment, and ensures that everybody's actions will be broadly predictable and sensible. More than anything, you have instilled a way of thinking about these things.

Another aviator to benefit from his prior experience was Captain Chesley Sullenberger, who landed US Airways Flight 1549 in the Hudson River, New York after ingesting geese in both engines shortly after take-off, in January 2009. All 155 passengers and crew survived and Sullenberger was lauded as a hero. Several commentaries have used the story of this accident to highlight lessons about communication or crew cooperation, but it always seemed to me that this was more than anything an example of clear thinking under pressure (see Chapter 5C) and that Sullenberger's previous military experience might be of more than passing relevance. In the context of the previous discussion on building the mental database, it is interesting to hear Sullenberger's own words: 'For 42 years, I've been making small, regular deposits in this bank of experience, education and training. And on January 15, the balance was sufficient that I could make a very large withdrawal.' As part of his military training, Sullenberger was a graduate of Exercise Red Flag. To come back to Napoloen, it is not genius . . .

Stress testing the assumptions

On 2 May 2011, a team of US Navy SEALs (special forces operatives), under the direction of the CIA, took off from Bagram Air Base in Afghanistan and, after a staging stop in Jalalabad, entered Pakistan en route to the suspected compound of Osama bin Laden, the leader of Al Qaeda, in Abbottabad. On arrival at the compound, one of the helicopters suffered a 'soft' crash landing due to an issue with localized airflow; however, the raid was still completed, during which time bin Laden was killed.

The raid was both politically and militarily fraught with risk. However, of all the many risks that would have been identified and mitigated (or accepted) in the planning of such a mission, one risk was identified as the single biggest factor in influencing whether the raid should go ahead or not. It may or may not be obvious to you, but the risk was whether it was actually bin Laden in the compound. The whole premise of the raid was a hypothesis, informed by multiple sources of data but still a hypothesis, that this was in fact bin Laden's base.

With that risk in mind, President Obama ordered a team to be formed, to take a fresh look at the evidence to support the hypothesis about the identity of the individual in the compound. Their brief was to come up with alternative hypotheses as to who else it might be. The team members had not been involved in any of the related intelligence operations up to that point, or in the planning of the raid; they were reviewing the evidence for the first time and had some significant reservations about the current hypothesis. The president reviewed the team's report in conjunction with his own team and security advisers and decided to authorize the raid.[6]

The Red Team

A team such as this is known as a 'Red Team' and its job is to stress test the assumptions in a plan or strategy, both during its development and during rehearsal of its execution, the latter sometimes in the context of 'wargaming'. The reason for, and value in, such a team is simple: objectivity. Most of us have a deeply ingrained fundamental flaw that we tend to get rather wedded to our own brilliance, and it simply doesn't occur to us that other people, who might be affected by our thinking and plans, or on whom our plans depend, might see the world from a different perspective. At the end of the twentieth century, Kodak was planning for success, not bankruptcy protection. The impending reality of the changing situation was not the key driver in its executives' thinking.

Red Teams are widely used by military and intelligence agencies to see an issue from a different perspective (often through the lens of an adversary or competitor) and to unpick the hidden assumptions in a strategy or plan; it is self-evident that the concept can also be highly valuable to other types of organizations.

The next level is to 'wargame' the execution in fast time. The wargame is a specific type of Red Team activity which allows us to put our plan to the test in an opposed role-play exercise so that we can *understand* and *anticipate* the likely outcomes, advantages and disadvantages of the plan, and if necessary *adapt* the plan in order to *win*. The output of the wargame is a greater understanding of how critical decisions may affect the outcome, and for those decisions to be made based on a judgement of acceptable risk. Additionally, tangible value can be delivered by allowing interdepartmental personnel to have clarity in common purpose and priority efforts, and to understand the wider context of their actions, and thereby synchronize their activities and make better collective decisions in the allocation of scarce shared resources.

This can be a remarkably fast and low-resource operation – it doesn't have to mean supercomputer modelling. The key personnel who will be responsible for the execution form the 'blue team', those chosen to represent the adversary's reactions form the 'red team', while other related (often neutral) parties are represented by the 'white team'. The plan is played out in rounds, with blue describing their plan and red and white their reactions. At the end of each round, the chairperson will highlight new tasks which have emerged, gaps in knowledge and risks for further investigation.

The ideal Red Team will contain three core types of people:

- **Operators.** People will extensive relevant operational experience who can simulate adversarial thinking.
- **Creatives thinkers.** Possibly people from a different operational domain, they will have no 'baggage' as to how things 'should be done' and offer a different perspective.
- **Analysts.** Intellectually rigorous thinkers who will challenge the underlying logic and assumptions.

This seems like a straightforward concept, and indeed it is. However, the successful deployment of Red Team type activities requires a certain objectivity and professionalism in organizational culture, where people are prepared to be challenged (and to learn) in the pursuit of excellence. You may find out some things you would have rather not had to hear, but for those who prefer to deal with truths head-on, and with a strong enough appetite for excellence, this can be a very powerful learning tool. It must be remembered that, in the final reckoning, the Red Team is actually on the same side and its aim is not to score points or make people look stupid, but to improve the likelihood of success.

Differential insight

The aim of the Red Team is to achieve a new insight, not achieved by others, which can make the difference between winning and losing. At business school I undertook an elective course in private equity, about half of which was taught by a current practitioner, who ran the European office of a large private equity company. Unsurprisingly, as somebody investing billions of other people's money in complex business deals, he was a first-class thinker; I found one of his key messages particularly useful. He was asked how it feels after closing a big deal: 'Champagne all round?' He said that he actually drives home and reflects that he has just paid more than anybody else in the world was prepared to pay for that business; he'd better know something that the others don't.

For him, apart from the requirement and ability to execute the plans for the business, the key issue in being comfortable with the fee paid was 'differential insight'. In his opinion, analysis of the data available was almost a functional task. It's a high-level functional task and requires some intellectually bright individuals but those people do exist and are not that rare a commodity. The bit that is actually really clever is what you do with the data, the ability to synthesize it and see something which offers a potential or value which others might not have seen.

A nice example of this is the story of Abraham Wald. Wald was a mathematics professor and was consulted during the Second World War to try and help reduce attrition to bomber aircraft because of enemy fire. Due to weight constraints, it was not possible to put additional armour over the whole aircraft and so it was planned to put more armour over the areas where returning aircraft had most damage. Wald disputed this plan and said that the additional armour should go on the areas that were most often undamaged. His thinking was that those aircraft that made it back with damage had nonetheless made it back. It seemed likely to him that it was when aircraft were hit in the areas that were undamaged on the returning aircraft that they would be shot down and fail to return. At the time, this was a drastic reinterpretation of the data.

I first read this story told second-hand by a social media executive in the context of 'big data'. His claim was that at his company (a global brand name), 'the thing we apply most is that there's a creative part to understanding quantitative data that requires a sort of artistic or creative approach.' I don't agree that the Wald example supports this conclusion. Wald did not make some leap that requires some abstract creative talent. He was a mathematics professor. I believe that he was actually being hyper-rational and unpicking the assumptions in the conclusions that others were reaching (that aircraft got shot down because they were hit in the areas that were most often damaged). Some will always be better than others at this sort of thinking, but Wald's skills are not an abstract quality; they are something that can be understood and potentially reproduced.

When it comes to planning, the correct framing of the issue and objective challenge of the underlying assumptions in our thinking can dramatically improve both the quality and apparent creativity of our solutions.

Leading a planning team

My description of planning in this chapter implicitly articulates a linear process conducted by a single team with one leader. In practice, of course, planning is carried out for complex cross-functional tasks by the same cross-functional teams mentioned in Chapter 4, with similar processes being replicated in parallel by teams at different levels, each with their own leader. Leading this process is different to being involved in the planning yourself. To paraphrase Field Marshal Montgomery, it is the leader's job to direct planning and make decisions, and for others to then work out the detail of those plans.

If I am the mission commander, I will initially digest the mission myself, perhaps with one or two of my inner team. Resources may well have already been allocated by a higher authority according to need, so I will see who and what I have got on my extended team. My first significant event is probably a mass brief for everybody involved, where the mission aim (what) is described together with the wider picture (why) and background intelligence.

We then commence the planning process. I will pull together the team leaders from the different elements and sub-teams allocated to the mission and brainstorm the mission, come up with an initial gameplan and send them away to start working on details with their own teams. I will try and maintain the discipline to avoid getting locked into details and concentrate on high-level management of the task and resources. My own squadron, almost by definition, will be providing the mission critical element – that is why the leader (me) has been selected from that squadron. However, I may not even lead my own sub-team, preferring to take a subordinate role, in order that I can concentrate on the overall mission, as opposed to my own team's specific task.

After a suitable time interval, I call my different element leaders together to review progress collectively. This process continues at appropriate intervals throughout the planning. That way everybody is updated on the 'big picture' and coordination or resource problems are highlighted early. If coordination with one of the elements is particularly critical to the mission, I may embed one of my team with that element, or the element leader might embed one of his team with me, such that there is a subject matter expert on hand to provide instant expertise and to help coordinate.

As the plan develops, we will also start to stress-test the contingencies and work through various major problems which might arise internally (e.g. unavailability of a critical asset), as well as modelling how the opposition might react to our actions, and what we in turn will do in order to maintain the initiative and the upper hand. At the final meeting, I will run through the overall plan at a high level, confirm understanding and take a final check for flaws. We are now ready to brief.

Summary of key points

- The real value is not the plan, but the planning
- Frame the issue; watch out for the right solution to the wrong problem
- The Mission Planning Process:
  - Aim – absolute clarity in what success looks like

- o Start at the end – be proactive rather than reactive; work backwards from the end
- o Analysis – what are we up against; what have we got going for us
- o Action plan – who will do what, when, why and how; play to relative strengths
- o Contingency – what's plan B? More than anything, it's a way of thinking
- Watch out for your own brilliance: stress-test your assumptions
- Avoid doing the work of one level down; in planning the leader's job is to direct, coordinate and align

Communicating the plan

How far would Moses have gone if he had taken a poll in Egypt?

Harry S. Truman

Which guns did you mean?

On 25 October 1854, one Major General James Brudenell, the 7th Earl of Cardigan (henceforth 'Cardigan') led his cavalry brigade in an attack against a well defended Russian position as part of the Battle of Balaclava, itself part of the Crimean War. The attack was a total failure. Of his 670 Troopers, 118 men were killed, 127 were wounded and 60 were taken prisoner. His commanding officer had intended him to attack a different position.

The bravery of the Cardigan's men is beyond doubt. The same is true of the (low) professional competence of the senior officers. The commander of the British forces was Lord Raglan, who was viewing proceedings from high ground some distance away. He observed the Russians trying to move some captured British guns, and sent an order via one Captain Nolan to the effect that the cavalry should advance rapidly to stop the guns being removed. However, the order was vague and unspecific, and assumed that the commander of the Cavalry, Lieutenant General George Bingham, the 3rd Earl of Lucan (henceforth 'Lucan') had the same view of what was happening, which he did not. From his position, Raglan was observing a situation that none of his units and officers on lower ground could see.

Lucan could only see one set of guns, a Russian position at the other end of a valley to him. He questioned Nolan, who said that the order was to attack immediately, and who, despite having knowledge of Raglan's intention, failed to communicate specifically what that was. Lucan therefore ordered Cardigan, the commander of the Light

Brigade, to conduct a frontal attack up the valley, even though this seemed an apparent suicide mission. The Light Brigade was a cavalry unit mounted on light, fast, unarmoured horses, optimized for reconnaissance and skirmishing, and for chasing forces in retreat. The Russians were entrenched with excellent views of the incoming forces and further supporting artillery on either side of the valley.

Cardigan and Lucan had a poor relationship, better described as outright enmity; they were brothers-in-law and had 30 years of history between them. Cardigan did not question Lucan's order, but simply led the assault. There are no records of any soldiers objecting to the order.

A poorly defined task, poor communication of the task via the messenger and the behavioural dynamics between the key players combined to form the backbone of one of best known disasters in British military history: The Charge of the Light Brigade.[1]

It is largely irrelevant whether the mission is correct or the plan is any good, if those responsible for them do not communicate clearly such that those tasked with execution know specifically what is expected of them and why. This example illustrates just a few of the reasons why communication and understanding can break down. Add in time pressure, different languages, organizational culture ('It's not what we do') and remote working, and the barriers to effective communication multiply exponentially. This chapter lays out a simple methodology and describes an example of where an equally simple approach has had a transformational impact.

The concept of briefing

There gets to be a point at which the time for discussion, brainstorming, challenging ideas and planning is over and it is time to get stuff done. You had your chance to argue your point, and either your input was incorporated or it wasn't. Either way, it is now time to unite behind a plan and start to implement. It is far, far better to unite behind an imperfect plan and execute well with a common approach to deliver the desired outcome, than to continue to debate, argue and pursue individual agendas and ideas in the pursuit of a perfect plan. Is there such a thing anyway? We'd like to have the best plan possible in order to stack the odds of success in our favour; however, we know that no plan survives its collision with the real world. Any of the spectrum of plans that would have worked was, by definition, good enough. Execution is the only thing on which you are ultimately measured.

However, even with an imperfect plan, it is critical that we have a common approach and are all pulling in the same direction; this is one of the key drivers of outstanding execution and this is where the brief comes in. Our experience is that teams and organizations do a lot of executing, sometimes interspersed with some planning. However, briefing and debriefing are surprisingly rare commodities. Briefing in particular is a relatively quick and easy win compared to debriefing; it really is a no-brainer as a driver of performance. If you're putting all that effort into defining task clarity, role clarity and the allocation of resources, you might as well make sure that everybody understands it.

Briefing is different to planning. That may well fall into the category of 'statements of the blindingly obvious', but the key point for me is that planning is a team game, whereas briefing is a leadership game. If I am leading on a task, I want all the brainpower engaged on the plan. It may be that somebody has to have the decision-making authority to choose between alternative approaches, but I want the highest number of quality options to choose from and all the relevant subject matter experts working on their own bits of the plan.

However, briefing is where the discussion stops and the leader confirms to the team what the final plan actually is. The communication of the plan can take many forms, but at a tactical level it's where the leader stands up in front of the team and defines the roles, responsibility and accountability for who will do what, when, why and how. This is the factual bit – the process. However, the conduct of the brief also offers a chance to set the professional standard, get people engaged and focused on the task, and at its best, to motivate and inspire. I guarantee that I would be able to tell you within 60 seconds of the start of a fighter mission brief whether the mission is likely to be a success or not, simply by the leader's manner. Did we start on time? Are they prepared? Do they project confidence and competence? If the answer to those questions is 'yes', we're off to a great start before a word is uttered.

The mechanics of briefing

A good brief is a statement of the mission and how it will be achieved, the execution normally being described in a chronological order. I will take you through a simple generic example, before looking in more detail at a fighter mission brief and some non-military applications. Consider first this simple model, used by many thousands of officer cadets over the years:

S ituation
M ission
E xecution
A ny questions
C heck understanding

This is a very simple catch-all briefing template, which can be refined or augmented as required.

Situation

This is the wider picture of what is going on around us. It provides context for our task and answers the question of 'why'.

Mission

The statement of the mission should align with all the previous comments about the definition of the aim and objectives. It is a clear concise statement of what is to be achieved. In a verbal briefing, it may be worth repeating it for emphasis. All of our subsequent actions should be driven by achieving this aim so put some focus on it and imprint it at the front of everybody's mind.

Execution

Now describe the plan to achieve the outcome. For something quite straightforward, you can just start at the beginning and work through to the end. For a more complex project, you might want to put some structure in place to break down the execution into more easily digested chunks.

Any Questions

Always allow time in your briefing process for questions. Questions from the team are not indicative of a bad brief (although a very high number of questions might indicate that one or both of the plan and the brief were lacking!). They demonstrate that the team has been listening and want to make sure that they have absolute clarity in their own minds about their roles. There is also the outside chance of a question highlighting some important issue which you haven't even thought of. If that happens and the issue is a potential showstopper, don't be too proud to admit it. 'Shooting the messenger', when everybody knows that it was a very good question, isn't going to do much for your credibility or the chance of accomplishing the mission.

Check Understanding

Finally, ask a few pertinent questions of team members to confirm that their understanding is the same as yours. In just the same way that questions from the team are not meant to undermine you, questions to team members are not to show them up or embarrass them. It is simply to provide an objective check that the critical actions and decision points have been understood the same by everyone. If you think about the example of operating fighters on a night mission, you will quickly see that there is more upside in checking this than downside in worrying about offending somebody. As the operational processes improve and the team becomes more used to the briefing concept, nobody will be worried about being asked a question; they would be more worried if you didn't. In any case, unless the task is particularly complex or dangerous, a few choice questions will normally suffice.

Fighter pilot mission brief

So having got the hang of the basics, let's take a look at a practical example that is a little more involved: the fighter pilot mission brief. My own template would probably look something like this:

Time check and roll call
Overview
Aim and objectives
Intelligence brief
Domestics
Execution
Communications plan
Contingencies and Losers
Questions
Check of understanding

Without worrying too much about the fine detail, let me quickly run through the logic of this brief, with a few explanatory comments.

Time check and roll call

I start *exactly* on time. Synchronizing watches may not be relevant in a lot of environments, but starting on time still sends a message about your professional standards. Check that everybody who needs to be present is there. I have no problem with somebody being represented by a deputy if necessary, but that person attends as the person they are representing. There is no dilution of responsibility or accountability.

Overview

Essentially the 'situation' from the SMEAC brief.

Aim and objectives

You've got it by now!

Intelligence brief

The overview is really just context. The intelligence brief goes into more detail on the resources and capabilities which you are up against, as well as providing the latest up-to-date assessments.

Domestics

These are all the administrative or ancillary issues. On a fighter mission, it would include call signs, take-off and landing details and refuelling, all the routine but still important things which we need to get right in order to be in good shape for the mission. It shouldn't take too long to cover this stuff but it is important that you get it right. A written summary will often be helpful.

Execution

Same as SMEAC. If I am just briefing my own team, this is straightforward. If I am leading something bigger and this is the brief for the whole mission, I will most likely ask the element leaders to say a few words on their individual plans so that everybody taking part has some visibility on what the other elements are up to and how it all ties together.

Communications plan

On a flying mission, the communication plan is a breakdown of who will be on what frequency when. More generically it is the part of the overall plan that defines the means by which information will be shared such that the right information gets to the right people at the right time while avoiding unnecessary overload. It is really part of the domestics and might be included at that point, although if the mission is complex, it may only make sense to people once they already have an understanding of the execution, hence the reason for it appearing here in the flow of events.

Contingencies

This section is subtly different to that practised by, for instance, the Red Arrows. The reason is that, in that case, you have a con-stituted team who all work together every day on a task which is relatively less reactive to external factors. So any discussion of contingencies tends to be about what if something goes wrong internally. On fighter jet operations, every mission will have unique aspects in terms of the task and combination of people and resources. It is possible that the mission changes dramatically from day to day. The most likely source of problems is that the adversaries don't do what they were supposed to do in the plan.

So the leader will model some of the more likely alternate scenarios and work through a decision matrix outlining different flows of events and what should happen in each case. Ultimately, tactical decision-making will be decentralized; however, it is important that elements understand their freedoms and constraints to act independently in reactive scenarios, and what other people are likely to be doing in those scenarios. This scenario modelling is a powerful driver of execution – see the next chapter.

As well as contingencies, it is necessary to cover a 'loser plan'; this refers to how the plan changes if some individual or key element is unable to take part (e.g. due to technical failure). Who is the Deputy Leader? What is the plan in the event of unserviceability within key elements? What are the minimum resource requirements to execute the mission? What if desirable but not essential resources are unavailable? How does the plan change?

Questions and check of understanding

This is, in essence, the same as the SMEAC brief. If I was just briefing my own team, I would include an emergency question at the end. If I am briefing the whole mission, most emergencies would be handled internally within sub-teams, so that question would be irrelevant. It would, though, be relevant to cover major collective emergencies and search and rescue. The key point is to keep the brief relevant at an appropriate level of detail for your audience.

Briefing – case study

Briefing really should be an easy win. It is simply a matter of communicating and confirming the strategy, intent or tactical plan prior to execution. If the team is co-located, this might be done face-to-face; however, video conference or other electronic communication, for example, email, can be effective when used well. It seems obvious that briefing will improve clarity and understanding, both of which will contribute to alignment and effectiveness of the project team. The best briefs will do more than simply convey information; they will also convey the confidence, motivation and inspiration to succeed. However, if you do no more than achieve improved understanding and clarity, that is already of significant value.

For an example of the potential value-addition, consider the World Health Organization (WHO) Surgical Safety Checklist. The format is simple and formulaic, and in fact comprises three checklists: one to be completed before the induction of anaesthesia, one before the actual surgical intervention and one at the end. You might argue that following a checklist is not quite a briefing, but the checklist is simply an aide-memoire to assist the surgeon in what is effectively a brief for the team. For example, the pre-surgery list comprises four simple sections and would take no more than a few minutes:

• Introductions by name and role
• Confirmation of patient and procedure *(situation and mission)*
• Anticipated critical events *(execution and contingencies)*
• Antibiotics and Imaging *('domestics' from the pilot brief)*

Not exactly rocket science? In January 2009, the Harvard School of Public Health published a review[2] of the pilot scheme for the checklist, which ran from October 2007 to September 2008 in eight hospitals, one in each of the following cities: Seattle, Toronto, London, Auckland, Amman, New Delhi, Manila and Ifakara. Highlights of the review included:

• Rate of major complications fell from 11 per cent to 7 per cent, a reduction of more than a third
• In-patient deaths following major operations fell by more than 40 per cent
• Reductions of equal magnitude in high-income and low-income sites
• By the time of publication of the review, four countries had already established nationwide programmes to implement the process in all operating rooms

A more recent independent review was published in the *British Journal of Anaesthesia* in May 2012 by Walker, Reshamwalla and Wilson.[3] That review confirmed the trends indicated in the original paper and focused in more depth on some of the underlying issues and benefits – for example, '… addressed communication difficulties by developing a checklist to facilitate structured inter-professional briefings before general surgical procedures. Data were collected prospectively pre- and post-implementation of the checklist. The mean number of communication failures per procedure declined from 3.95 before the intervention to 1.31 after the intervention. Thirty-four per cent of briefings demonstrated utility, and the checklist also demonstrated associated improvements in situational awareness, decision-making, team working and reliability of clinical interventions . . . '.

It's amazing how performance can be improved simply by taking a few minutes to ensure that everybody knows what's going on . . .

Summary of key points

- The brief is the point at which the constructive challenge of the planning process ceases and the team unite behind a single course of action
- Planning is a team game but briefing is a team leader game
- At the simplest level, the brief just confirms the situation, the mission or task, and key elements of the execution
- Clarity and confirmation of understanding is a quick win in improving performance

Execution

Plans are simply good intentions unless they immediately degenerate into hard work.

Peter Drucker, US management thought leader

Friction and information overload

With a great plan and a great brief, how hard can execution be? Well, if you worked within the Soviet state system before perestroika, you could argue that it shouldn't be that difficult. Notwithstanding any fundamental weaknesses that might exist in system design, plans or leadership, there are very few external variables which are not planned for. Most are known and within the control of the state system. Just execute the plan.

In other less controlled systems, however, we are routinely executing with imperfect information and making decisions faced with ambiguity. The cascading of 'what' our task is, and 'why', is often far less clear than is ideal, and there are significant variables outside our control, not least the actions of other (potentially competitive) players in the same space, in addition to the economic or operating environment. And even if we do everything we can to address those issues through setting clear strategy and intent, clear communication through directives, and empowering people to take ownership of delivery, we are still ultimately reliant on individuals to deliver. Those individuals do not operate in some cotton wool-wrapped perfect world with plenty of spare mental capacity to get everything done right first time.

However, getting it 'right first time' is what we are trying to achieve. The only reason that we design, organize and try to inspire teams and organizations, and the reason that we invest time and effort in planning and briefing is to get something done, to achieve a purpose. The essence of the barrier to getting it right first time can be summed up as friction – the inconvenient effect of the real world.

Imagine you are working on a big project and you are close to personal capacity. If I keep adding more and more to your workload, there will eventually be some sort of failure or breakdown. Something gets missed; a ball gets dropped. The problem here is the ability to deal with information overload, to maintain focus on delivery and prioritize what will be truly important in delivering decisive success, with a thousand other issues competing for your attention. In this chapter, I describe an approach to achieve just that.

Priorities: What's the ball you can't afford to drop?

Before looking at an aviation example, consider first the main issues which a fast-jet pilot needs to deal with, illustrated in Figure 5.3.

She needs to fly her own aircraft, look after her formation (her team) and deal with the immediate tactical issue, at the same time as keeping

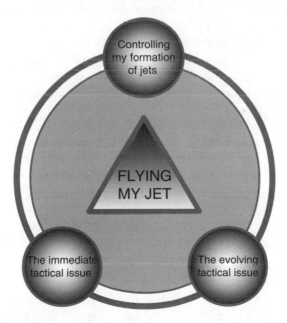

Figure 5.3 Aviation priorities

one eye (or ear!) on the wider evolving tactical situation. Now in a relatively low arousal sortie, that is all fine. It's what you train for. You can juggle all these balls, shifting your focus according to the relative priorities, keeping all the balls in the air, and still have some brainpower left.

However, now imagine that the workload and distractions pick up. It's proving difficult to stay on top of everything and maintain focus. Well, let's drop the evolving tactical situation. You don't want to drop it for too long, but it will be fine just to focus on the immediate priorities for a few minutes. Now it gets busier still. Let's drop the monitoring of the formation (the team); they can probably look after themselves anyway. Now even more things start to happen. I am in a 60-degree dive at 2,000ft (600m) at night. I will hit the sea in 1.75 seconds. Drop the immediate tactical issue. Fly the plane. No matter how busy I get, that's the ball that I cannot afford ever to drop.

Consider an example that we use as a case study. It describes an aircraft accident involving a Harrier aircraft. The Harrier is the 'jump jet' that can land vertically. In the case study (it is a real-life example, and I should point out that the pilot survived), a Harrier is coming back to land on an aircraft carrier in the Mediterranean. The sequence of events in landing on an aircraft carrier is that the aircraft starts by slowly descending to hover alongside the ship. It then moves across to hover above the deck, before finally descending vertically onto the deck. In this example, the pilot came alongside the aircraft carrier, never really stabilized and crashed in the sea.

Why did that happen? Before addressing that question, you should bear in mind the context. First, the accident happened at night, the ship had no lights on, and the pilots were flying with night-vision goggles. The pilot was therefore landing on a short strip of metal and concrete floating around in the middle of the ocean in pitch darkness while looking through a set of goggles that have all the depth perception and panoramic vision of looking through of a pair of toilet roll tubes. There is probably no greater pure skill challenge in aviation than landing on an aircraft carrier at night. And that is before you turn the lights off. Second, the pilot was just returning from a sortie and had insufficient fuel to divert to a land base, so he was committed to landing on the aircraft carrier. Finally, he was also the squadron boss. In addition to the pressures of the functional task, he also had a myriad of management and leadership issues on his agenda, all waiting for him as soon as he landed. There were a lot of things competing for this pilot's attention.

During the descent to the ship, the safety pilot (on the ship) commented several times to the pilot that the approach was high. However, the pilot still attempted to stabilize alongside the aircraft carrier, reducing power to adjust his position as he did so. The aircraft started to descend further and reached a situation where its downwards momentum was such that even full engine power was insufficient to reverse the descent. The aircraft crashed into the sea. During the approach of the aircraft to the ship, the safety pilot could be heard providing an increasing volume of advice with escalating urgency, but unfortunately, the pilot's ability to process additional inputs (often hearing) was, by that point, almost certainly at capacity. He didn't apply additional power until it was too late and the aircraft crashed.

Why did that happen? Well, we can't say for certain what thoughts and decisions were going through that pilot's mind immediately prior to the accident but we can say with some confidence that he dropped the 'fly the plane' ball. After all, notwithstanding the intrinsic challenge in the night approach, the pilot had the skills, training and experience to be able to do just that. He had done it lots of times before. Why not this time? The problem with information overload and loss of focus is that it is often insidious. It just creeps up on you and catches you unawares. You don't mean to miss the target; you don't mean to be late for a meeting; he didn't mean to crash into the sea.

Recognizing overload

One potential solution is in developing the ability to recognize your own symptoms. You might have some specific personal reactions to stress or it might be as simple as feeling totally 'maxed out.' You just don't know where to start on anything. Recognize the symptom, close the door, turn off your email and think for a minute. What are we actually trying to achieve? What are the priorities? What's the ball you can't afford to drop? During a particularly busy period at Mission Excellence, I wrote our priorities on a board in the office:

1. Client delivery
2. Sales pipeline
3. Everything else

We should always prioritize above anybody else those people who have already committed to give us money in return for a deliverable. Next, we should be worried about communicating with our pipeline of future prospects. And we shouldn't really be worrying too much about administrative issues, unless the first two are under control. Of course, there are exceptions to the above – for example, accounts need to be filed on time – but consistently applying the general principle will normally stand us in good stead.

An interesting corollary to the Harrier accident story was the reaction of the wingman when he saw the accident happen. On the video taken from his cockpit, you clearly hear him say 'Oh, my God,' and then the same thing again: 'Oh, my God'. Bear in mind that, at that moment, he believed that he had just watched his boss die. He then proceeded to have a completely routine discussion with the air traffic controller on the ship about the fact that he had no fuel to divert and would be performing one circuit around the ship before landing. It would be difficult to find a better example of somebody deliberately choosing which balls to drop. Can you imagine the stress and emotion that the wingman was feeling at that time? However, he clearly focused on the one single overriding priority: fly the plane. Land back on the ship.

The ship's captain came out of the incident similarly well. Picture the scene on the bridge. There was an aircraft in the water. We need to launch search and rescue, turn the ship around. None of those things happened. The ship just kept going in the same direction. There was another aircraft still in the air on low fuel. The priority was to recover that aircraft first. This is another great example of absolute clear thinking and focus under pressure. Once the wingman had landed, the ship did turn around, rescued the pilot, and amazingly was also able to recover the aircraft almost immediately, which was floating on the surface.

Know the ball that you can't afford to drop.

Execution and the art of decision-making

The aim of the performance model underpinning this book is to describe a series of factors, which when correctly addressed and sequenced, give us the maximum chance of delivering high performance:

1. **People.** Organizations which rely on team activities require People with team-based values and behaviours, to which best-in-class functional and non-technical skills must be added.
2. **Capability.** To give this group of people the best chance of succeeding, we need to build Capability through clarity in 'what' and 'why', high degrees of alignment and commonality in approach and the freedom to do what is required, within defined boundaries, to deliver the desired outcome.
3. **Delivery.** And finally individual tasks and projects are planned and briefed for Delivery with a laser-like focus on the outcome.

As we have seen in this chapter, even if we get all of the above factors about right, the real world has a nasty habit of intruding on our activities. The critical success factor in execution may rest on our subjective decision-making, when faced with something different to what was planned for. In his book *Blink*,[1] Malcolm Gladwell contrasts the relative benefit of extensive rational analysis by an informed layperson with the intuitive opinion of an expert, and asks how it is that an expert can make a judgement call to reach an opinion in a fraction of the time required for the associated analysis. At the risk of completely failing to do justice to Gladwell's bestseller, he offered the argument (my words) that an expert has an internal mental model formed subconsciously over years and years of experience that can be instantly compared with the issue or problem at hand.

Gladwell's hypothesis makes sense, but, in my opinion, there is more to the issue than the passive explanation that we learn by osmosis because we have seen something before, and then over time we form a mental model which we can utilize semi-automatically as a comparison with what we are seeing.[2] What I have tried to describe over the preceding chapters is a rather more active approach to improving decision-making. Consider three scenarios:

1. **Known Knowns.** Scenarios that we can reasonably assume might occur can be planned for in advance. If they are common, we don't want to be wasting time and capacity on every occasion that they arise, so we include the appropriate actions in the SOPs (Chapter 4). A variant is any situation that we can anticipate occurring that requires a perfect or time-critical response. For those, we can use checklists. In both examples, we have effectively scripted our decision-making and thereby retained our spare mental capacity for more ambiguous situations requiring original thought and/or judgment.

2. **Known Unknowns.** Scenarios that we can foresee as a possibility but without detailed definition are dealt with through scenario planning – for example:
   a. Simulation
   b. Red Teaming
   c. Wargaming
   d. Contingency planning
   All of these activities are, to some degree, making small regular deposits in Captain Sullenberger's bank of experience, education and training from Chapter 5A. We don't know when we will need to make a withdrawal or for what purpose, but by building up a lot of credit in the bank, we give ourselves a greatly increased chance of making a good decision in the heat of the moment, compared to the situation where we have never even considered a similar scenario.

3. **Unknown Unknowns.** The things that will really ruin our day, however, are the unknown unknowns that we simply didn't see coming. Some or all of the factors in the previous two paragraphs may still be relevant and helpful in those situations, but when faced with increasing complexity and reducing time, our best ever decision will be 'about right, now'. It's a new scenario and there is no time for analysis; we need clear simple priorities to fall back on. What's the ball you can't afford to drop?

Case study – Marks and Spencer

I was trying to shake up a culture of paralysis. Hiding behind data or precedents to avoid making a decision had to stop. If it looks like a duck and it quacks like a duck, you don't need to send it for DNA testing to find out six months later it's a duck. Take a risk, guys; it's a duck.

Lord Rose of Monewden

I highlighted in Chapter 1 that my approach is empirical, based on experience of what works. One can never model the complex system of the 'real world' perfectly but by reversing engineering the methodology, one can avoid some of the significant assumptions in a purely theoretical approach. Most people are not asked to deliver results within a closed system over which they have total control. The relevant benchmark for any model is whether it works when playing a less than ideal hand and simultaneously dealing with the friction of customers, competitors and other parties whose interests may not be aligned. Consider the performance of British retailer, Marks and Spencer (M&S) in 2004–2007.[3]

History

M&S is a British retailing icon occupying a unique place in the heart of the British consumer, in particular for female shoppers; it has over 1,330 stores worldwide. Following poor performance in the late 1990s, a new CEO was installed. Six years, two CEOs and two chairmen later in May 2004, M&S was being touted as an ideal candidate for a leveraged buyout. On Thursday, 27 May 2004, Philip Green made his move. On Monday, 31 May, Paul Myners was installed as chairman and Stuart Rose as CEO. Rose had only a matter of days to formulate his plans to convince shareholders that there was more value in the business than Green was offering, at the same time as bringing in a new management team to run the business, not to mention the minor issue of turning around performance.

Rose did have the advantage of both knowing the business well, having worked in M&S from 1972 to 1989, and being an external recruit in 2004, unconnected to the current team. He also brought his key lieutenants, Charles Wilson (Operations) and Steve Sharpe (Marketing), with him, with Rose initially looking after Product himself. It was still a demanding challenge by any measure though. The plan for the turnaround had to be developed fast and to be convincing enough to defeat the bid. Rose led a diagnostic phase that aimed to bring simplicity and clarity to the issues. He concluded that M&S had simply lost touch with its customers, its heritage and core values. On 12 July, Rose presented his turnaround plan to analysts. The thrust of his message was 'back to basics' and focused on:

- Product
- Service
- Environment (store improvement)

He committed to return to M&S' core values and outlined a plan with 3 phases:

- Focus (04/05): re-establish basic retail standards and satisfying core customers
- Drive (05/06): substantial improvements in product, service, store layout and supply chain
- Broaden (06/07): appeal to a wider UK customer base and build on the successful international franchise business

On 14 July nearly 3,000 small shareholders offered almost total support to the Board at the M&S annual meeting in London and Green dropped his bid. Rose and his team implemented their plan. After taking a lot of upfront cost in the first year under Rose, UK retail sales were down 1.7 per cent and group profit down 19 per cent. However by the half-year interim results in November 2005, the pendulum was starting to swing. UK sales were down 0.2 per cent while group operating profit was up 27.1 per cent. Most importantly during Q2 (the second quarter), clothing, the key part of the M&S value proposition, showed a 0.2 per cent like-for-like increase. This was the start of a period of continuous performance improvement until the top of the cycle in mid-2007. During the subsequent financial crash, M&S suffered the same woes as its competitors, but did outperform them in the some of worst trading conditions in living memory.

Lessons

I interviewed Rose in 2009 and again in 2015, while doing research for this book. It is instructive to group some of his reflections by the factors within our high-performance model:

1. **People**.
   a. *Values, Behaviours and Skills*. I asked Rose which he considered more important: the functional competency of his executive team or the

dynamic between the individuals. He responded that best-in-class competency was simply a prerequisite. The point of difference was their ability to combine effectively together.

b. *Trust*. Rose also highlighted that knowing the other person's competence and commitment to the cause facilitated trust, which was essential to success. Micromanagement was not an option (see below).

2. **Capability.**

a. *Clarity*. Clarity is a key theme of any discussion with Rose whether describing the concept of retail: 'we buy for one pound, and hopefully sell for two', or his focus on the basics. Despite the scale of the challenge, he decluttered rather than cluttered. Rose was also keen to point out the importance of role clarity; each of the executive team had a clearly defined area of responsibility.

b. *Alignment*. Before Rose, the business had become highly decentralized without accountability and central strategy. Rose reinstated a common approach and centralized strategy but not execution. He insisted on measuring what was actually important with clear lines of accountability and alignment of reward. Information sharing was regular and effective with 'morning prayers' held daily during the bid defence[4] together with a brief end of day summary. The executive team were constantly available to each other. The primary medium was face-to-face ('just come and talk to me'). Minutes were not required and email was only used for this purpose by exception.

c. *Empowerment*. Rose commented that with so much going on, he would have struggled to micromanage the executive team, never mind the thousands of other employees.

3. **Delivery**. On taking over as CEO, Rose had one weekend to review the books. In his own words: 'I had a look at the figures just to check that there was no smoking black hole. To be honest, I would have probably taken the job no matter what I found; I just wanted to understand how big the problem was.'

a. *Planning*. Rose started with an analysis of the status quo and the current market before focusing on M&S' traditional strengths and committing to a plan which leveraged those strengths to maximum effect. However, Rose knew that his stakeholders would not wait for ever and also planned for some quick wins. Overlaid with the business recovery planning was a highly reactive daily planning cycle to defend against the bid.

b. *Communication of the Plan*. Communication of the plan is different to the internal information sharing described above. One of Rose's mantras was 'communicate, communicate, communicate'. He proactively engaged through PR, briefings to analysts and meetings with management, staff and customers. The plan and its inherent priorities were clear to one and all.

c. *Execution*. Rose was acutely aware of the danger of noise and management speak crowding out what was truly important and he never wavered from his three simple priorities: product, service and environment. In fact, one of his few regrets is that he didn't focus on those things even more and move faster to upgrade stores. Clear simple priorities allowed everyone from the executive team to the cashier to know what was the ball they couldn't drop.

4. **Leadership**. We will cover leadership in Chapter 7, however it is worth making a few pre-emptive comments here. While different reviewers have widely differing opinions on exactly how much of the success in that period was down to Rose alone (something he would definitely not claim), certain aspects of his actions and behaviours appear to have added significant positive value:

a. *Leading from the front*. While at subsequent analyst presentations, Rose shared the load, at his first big test in presenting the Operational Review in July 04, Rose owned the stage from beginning to end and accepted personal responsibility to deliver a share price of £4.

b. *Symbolism*. Rose sent skips to stores to clear out old signage (a clear break with the past), returned cash to shareholders immediately after defeating Green's bid, used his own (M&S) clothes at presentations to illustrate quality and value for money and with the food business initially in better shape, ran a highly engaging food advertising campaign before there was any real sign of recovery.

c. *Passion*. The most successful leaders of retail businesses invariably wear their passion for the product and the business on their sleeve. Both Green and Rose were genuine product experts and huge brand advocates.

Implicit in much of what has just been said is the agility to react to events and to apply learning fast. This is the subject of the next chapter.

Conclusion

Every chapter up to this one has been about putting in place the enablers of high performance: the individual attitudes, standards and values; the recruitment and development of team players; empowering agility and execution through clarity, alignment and empowerment; the application of a discipline in planning in order to drive decisive success; and the briefing of a plan such that it is cascaded with clarity. All this does, though, is to stack the odds in your favour; people still have to deliver. In this chapter, we have looked at execution – the things the organization can do to prepare the individual and the team, and the key issues for both individuals and teams in defeating information overload. Next we need to look at the key to sustainable performance and continuous improvement – learning, and the way we debrief.

Summary of key points

- With many factors outside your control, things will rarely work out as planned
- The more complex the situation, the simpler the priorities need to be: 'fly the plane'
- Know the ball that you can't afford to drop
- Information overload:
  - Recognize your symptoms
  - Prioritize
  - Deliberately focus your attention on the right place at the right time
- The art of decision-making:
  - SOPs for scenarios you can define and anticipate being common
  - Scenario modelling for situations which are possible but lack definition
  - Clear priorities for swerveballs

Chapter 6

Accelerating performance (Learning)

Experience is what you get when you didn't get what you wanted.
Randy Pausch

An organization with a memory

Large organizations that operate in safety-critical environments tend to be easy targets for those who wish to throw spears. Things will never be perfect and their bad experiences are often in the public domain. The United Kingdom's National Health Service (NHS) is no exception. It's a supertanker of an organization, reportedly in the top five largest in the world by number of employees,[1] alongside the US Department of Defence, McDonald's, Walmart and the People's Liberation Army in China. It employs more than 1.6 million people and provides free healthcare services to a population of 65 million.

The fact that this system works at all is a great example of exceptional team and organizational performance. That many, or even most, of its users receive excellent healthcare service is nothing short of a miracle. In 2014, the Commonwealth Fund declared that in comparison with the healthcare systems of ten other countries (Australia, Canada, France, Germany, Netherlands, New Zealand, Norway, Sweden, Switzerland and the United States), the NHS was the most impressive overall. The NHS was rated as the best system in terms of efficiency, effective care, safe care, coordinated care, patient-centred care and cost-related problems. I do plan to use the NHS here for some examples of things that haven't gone so well, but my spears should be viewed in the context of the size of the task and the overall achievement.

Like many large organizations, learning from experience is not the NHS' greatest strength. Implementing a culture of learning, and systemizing the knowledge management systems to share and apply that learning, has proved to be an elusive goal. However, to fail to learn is to commit to making the same mistakes next time.

The Donaldson report

In 2000, the then NHS Chief Medical Officer, Sir Liam Donaldson, chaired a group on learning from adverse events that produced a seminal report on patient safety, entitled 'An Organization with a Memory'.[2] There follows an example of sort of the material contained within the report:

- Between 1985 and 2000, at least thirteen cases occurred in the United Kingdom of people being killed or paralysed due to maladministration of drugs by spinal injection. The circumstances in most cases were very similar.
- In twelve of these cases, the drug should never have been given by spinal injection. At least ten were fatal.
- The drugs in question had been in use since the 1950s and the consequences of spinal injection were known, however no central record of incidents was ever created.
- In a 1997 case, manslaughter charges were brought against two doctors involved in an example of the above; the case received wide media attention (although the charges were eventually dropped). The following year, a further fatal case occurred.

Every aspect of the above sequence indicates that learning was being neither captured nor applied. While Donaldson's report was in some ways more akin to an inquiry than self-learning by the protagonists, and came too late for many, it subsequently did provide a powerful example of the capability to apply learning. After the publication of the report, new procedures were introduced and the National Reporting and Learning System (NHS incident database) was set up. There have been no reported deaths for this reason in the United Kingdom since 2001.

As well as the individual tactical examples, Donaldson and his group also commented on the organizational culture:

Learning culture 5.8
Our review of the current position confirms that there are several key areas in which the NHS falls short of being a learning organization at the outset. There is too often a 'blame' culture. When things go wrong, the response is often to seek one or two individuals to blame, who may then be subject to disciplinary measures or professional censure. That is not to say that in some circumstances individuals should not be held to account, but as the predominant approach this acts as a significant deterrent to the reporting of adverse events and near misses. It also encourages serious underestimation of the extent to which problems are due not to individuals but to the systems in which they operate.

Many of the observations had associated recommendations, in this case Recommendation 3 (Encourage a reporting and questioning culture in the NHS):

We recommend that the NHS should encourage a reporting culture amongst its staff which is generally free of blame for the individual reporting error or mistakes, and encourage staff to look critically at their own actions and those of their teams. We acknowledge that significant progress has been made in this area in recent months and years, but believe that there is scope for further action in a number of key areas.

The Francis report

In 2013, Robert Francis produced his report on the failings at the Mid Staffordshire NHS Foundation Trust (essentially a major hospital) between 2005 and 2009. Conditions of appalling care were able to flourish at the hospital. The report identified that the culture was not conducive to providing good care for patients or a supporting environment for staff; there was an atmosphere of fear and a high priority was placed on the achievement of targets, as opposed to care or safety (again: you get what you reward). Francis' report was damning, but most tellingly in the context of this chapter, he wrote in the introduction: 'The evidence to this enquiry has shown that we have still not managed to move successfully away from the culture of blame which Professor Sir Liam Donaldson, in *An Organization with a Memory* and Professor Sir Ian Kennedy, in the report of *The Bristol Inquiry*, were so keen to banish'.

Other sectors

It is only fair to point out that the issues above are not peculiar to the NHS or the sector. My own previous employer, the RAF, makes learning and safety genuine priorities within the organization. The apparent relative success of those initiatives at the tactical level did little to protect the organization from strategic level failings. Charles Haddon-Cave subtitled his 2009 report into the loss of fourteen lives due to the explosion of a Nimrod aircraft in Afghanistan: 'A Failure of Leadership, Culture and Priorities',[3] a phrase which tells its own story. Among the many observations and lessons was that a very similar incident to the one which caused the fatal accident had occurred previously, but which had only resulted in a near miss. The tragedy is that the benefit of the potential learning from the near miss was never exploited; there was no system in place to connect the dots and that no one was actually responsible for doing so.

The Macondo accident in the Gulf of Mexico is considered the worst oil spill in history. In addition to the environmental disaster, eleven people lost their lives. The spill began with an explosion on 20 April 2010, and the subsea well was not capped until 15 July of the same year. During that time the US government estimates that 4.9mn barrels of oil were discharged into the ocean.[4] The subsequent investigation was carried out by a Presidential Commission, which identified a myriad of contributory factors to the accident. However, one of the most shocking revelations to emerge from this tragedy was that a near miss with the same underlying technical issues had occurred only a few months before in the North Sea on a well called Bardolino. In his paper 'The Macondo Inflow Test Decision ...',[5] Dr John Thorogood notes: 'Detailed accounts of near miss events from which learnings might be taken are hard to come by in the drilling domain.' It may be that this is not due to an absence of near miss events, but more often because the learning is simply not done or disseminated.

A culture of learning

Why do organizations fail to learn? One major barrier is the investment of time and effort required. It's another credit into Captain

Sullenberger's bank and you simply don't know if or when the future debit will be required, which makes it difficult to justify the investment in the first place. Chapter 5A opened with a quote to the effect that it's more fun to do stuff than spend time planning. The same is true for learning, only100 times more so. At least planning and briefing offer quick wins. They will shortly be followed by execution, when the benefits of a good plan and brief should immediately become obvious. Investing in learning is the same as investing in non technical training and skill acquisition – it's a leap of faith (Chapter 3).

For that reason, when faced with competing priorities for our time, learning is an easy one to move down the list below the next delivery. Culture can also be a significant barrier. We have done extensive work in the Middle and Far East. As one travels further east from Europe, one starts to observe increasing deference to age and seniority, something which can be very positive in a family or a community. However, the way in which that can play out in practice in the professional environment is that nobody challenges upwards or tells the boss bad news. This is not ideal; the boss is the last person to ever find out about the impending disaster. We have done a lot of work with the British oil industry in Aberdeen. On average, the offshore element of the UK oil industry seems to be dominated by tough, middle-aged men. They are exactly the sort of people you need to do difficult, demanding work in dangerous conditions. But they are perhaps not the best cross section for doing a bit of soul searching about where they need to improve.

Add in organizational demographics, language issues, ego and hierarchy, and there are a lot of good reasons not to prioritize some of the difficult conversations required to make learning from experience into a reality. However, if you don't actively learn from experience, how will you stop yourself from making the same mistakes next time as last time? Lots of organizations talk about being learning organizations and learning from experience, but you have to do something to capture the learning, otherwise you just get better by osmosis, because you're older and you've done it before. In high-performance environments, people don't just talk about learning and continuous improvement; they actually do something to make it happen.

The debrief

I place Learning at the centre of the high-performance model, introduced in Chapter 1 at Figure 1.3, because it is the key factor pervading
all aspects of high performance and the pursuit of excellence: personal
development, self-awareness and mastery of skills (People); improving
communication processes and internal alignment (Capability); and
learning from operational experience (Delivery). In my experience,
there are three critical success factors in accelerating learning and
performance: humility (an acceptance of the potential to learn), drive
(a desire to improve) and objectivity (the ability to park one's ego and
make the review process as evidence-based as possible). Humility and
drive are both values at some level, although one could argue that
drive is the behavioural evidence of some deeper value. Either way,
I don't plan to try and provide much further insight into them here
and now. However, we will discuss objectivity at some length later in
this chapter.

The focus here is the capture and application of learning from operational experience, both how we do that and how we make it as objective as possible. This is different to a learning and development process
or learning a new functional skill. It is learning on the job in real time,
and applying it swiftly to drive performance improvement. The primary example used is the debrief – the review that occurs at the end of a
task or project, or at some key milestone. In the context of delivery, the
debrief is where we close the execution cycle:

Plan – Brief – Execute – Debrief.

What is a debrief?

When I present on high-performance teams and debriefing, I usually
ask the audience how many of them take part in a regular debrief and
I frame the word in a very specific way: 'This is not an HR process or a
line management process, where somebody has a monopoly on being
right (or thinks they do!) and the feedback is one-directional; this is
a regular objective assessment of team performance where there is no
seniority involved, and the leader might learn as much as anyone else
in the room.' Framed like that, very few people usually feel confident

enough to put their hand up to claim that they debrief regularly, especially in front of their peer group, who might have some insight into, and comment on, what really goes on!

What actually is a debrief? At Mission Excellence, we define it as follows:

A debrief is an objective assessment of team performance against a plan, carried out by the team themselves, ideally at the end of a time-bounded period of activity with a defined outcome.

We will discuss all the aspects of this in a lot more detail, but just to pick up on a few key points here:

- **Objective assessment:** This is perhaps the single biggest challenge to self-analysis.
- **Team performance:** We explore team debriefs here, since they are the more difficult scenario and often where the biggest value lies; however, the same underlying principles apply to everything from one-person endeavours to organizational performance.
- **Against a plan:** We don't just explore how things went; we explore how things went against how we planned for them to go. It's important to remember that the debrief is just one part of the execution cycle and doesn't work as well in isolation. If there was no clear aim or plan, it's going to be quite hard to debrief, because there was no clarity or agreement in what we set out to do. Also, even with a plan, we could have a great result for completely the wrong reasons or simply because we got lucky; we'd like to know if that is the case, because we probably won't get lucky twice.
- **Carried out by the team themselves:** See below on the difference between feedback and debriefing. In short, only the people who 'did the doing' can truly know the real reasons for why they did what they did. Other parties can only offer their observation or their perception, that is, feedback.
- **Time-bounded period of activity with a defined outcome:** In the same way that we debrief against the plan, we really want to debrief against the outcome. There's no point congratulating ourselves on a brilliantly executed plan if we completely failed to achieve the end game. This will be difficult to define if there was no real start or end

to the activity. As an aside, even for 'business as usual' it is still often possible to satisfy this criterion by careful choice of parameters.

A little bit of history

It is difficult to define one continuous thread in the development of debriefing practice. Many operational parts of the military will practice some form of debriefing, and the US Army appears to have staked some claim to be the originator of After Action Review (AAR), at least in academic literature.[6] The AAR is one form of debrief that, by virtue of its very simple generic approach, can be easily applied to many environments, although it does have some limitations.

Outside of the military AAR often only occurs when something went wrong. The issue then is that it's going to be a lot more difficult to have a good quality open honest conversation if the process is not a routine event and only associated with failure and blame. Another issue I have observed is that only specific individuals become qualified to conduct AARs. While this ensures objectivity, it is going to be far more difficult for someone external to a task (and possibly with limited functional insight and credibility) to unpick the truth about why things happened in the way they did.

The sort of self-managed routine debriefing that I have in mind is particularly prevalent in fast-jet aviation (and also special forces, although I have less personal insight here). I believe that there are two reasons for that. The first is the dangerous nature of the operating environment, in which failing to learn from experience can have up close and personal consequences; can we afford not to debrief? The second is that, as a result of the first reason, an organizational culture has developed in fast-jet aviation where debriefing has simply become the norm. On the Red Arrows, there is also a third reason, which is the training burden. With a 33 per cent turnover rate of display pilots, the team needs the ability to achieve a rapid continuous improvement every year, and it is the employment of an iterative learning cycle that empowers this; each debrief provides the learning and the focus for the next sortie.

I would assume that debriefing has, to some extent, probably always been present in military aviation, although the modern focus can be traced back to Vietnam. In that conflict, the US Air Force (USAF) losses were significantly higher than might reasonably have been predicted, which forced the USAF into a period of soul-searching about its training and preparation of fighter pilots for combat. The end result was the development of Exercise Red Flag at Nellis Air Force Base in Nevada, described in Chapter 4. A key component of Red Flag is learning, and it is common for the debrief to last as long as the mission. There is an analogy here with exercise, where muscle development actually occurs in the rest after the exercise. In human endeavour, the performance improvement often comes in the reflection after the task.

I believe that much of the best practice in this field is from the military, but it's definitely not exclusively a military issue. Listen to any of the high performers previously mentioned – for example, Sebastian Coe, Dave Brailsford and Clive Woodward – and you will hear similar stories.

What a debrief isn't

Before diving into the 'how' of debriefing, it is also useful to understand what a debrief isn't. The diagram in Figure 6.1 illustrates four different types of review process. As you move around the circle from assessment to debrief, each stage involves an ever-increasing element of equality of the players, the discussion and analysis becoming ever more of a two-way street, moving from a scenario where one person knows the 'correct' answer and simply assesses the other person, to a scenario where nobody knows the learning outcome until the activity has collectively been analysed. The diagram can also be split down the middle. The right-hand side refers to externally owned and controlled activities; those on the left-hand side are internally owned and controlled.

- Assessment is what it says. A third party conducts some sort of independent assessment of competence. It tends to occur in educational and training establishments, and in other environments where there is some sort of qualification representing skill acquisition.

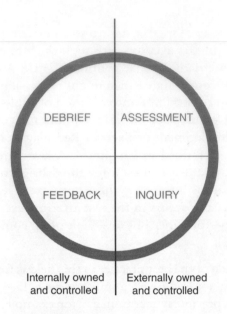

Figure 6.1 Types of performance review

- Inquiry tends to happen when something goes wrong: the aircraft crashes or you lose a big contract. An independent party conducts an inquiry to establish the root causes of some sort of adverse event. While there is sometimes a lot of noise about learning, the reality is often that this process is about establishing accountability and blame.
- Feedback happens where one party effectively has a monopoly on being right, where the feedback flows in only one direction from the 'expert' to the less experienced. It tends to imply sort of experience or ability gradient; personal annual reports might be an example. One other important type of feedback discussed below is client feedback.
- Debrief is a collective assessment of team performance where everybody is equal and everybody is there to learn.

It is useful to think about the difference between feedback and debrief as just defined. Feedback is what you get from your client or customer and so on; debrief is what you do with that information. We have met a lot of people who talk about debriefing with their clients. However,

I tend to be quick to point out that you can't debrief with your client, because your client doesn't know why you did what you did; they can only comment on the outcome or their perception. It is important to note that your client's perception at this point is effectively a fact. There's no point in retrospectively trying to change their opinion. Their perception *is* their reality. What is more important is to gather as much data and insight as possible from your client – that is, their *feedback* – and then to go away and ask yourself *(debrief)* what did we do (and why) that got the client to that place, and whether the work was won or lost, how you could do it better next time, and so on. You have to own the outcome that happened; there is little point in blaming somebody else.

Debrief behaviours

When talking about the practicalities of debriefing, I tend to start with behaviours for two reasons. First, the behaviours required in a debrief are a great example of the sort of behaviours that drive team performance far more generally. And second, although I tend to think that behaviours and process carry equal weighting in a successful debrief, the reality is that it is often far more difficult to embed the right behaviours than it is to improve the process.

In order to illustrate the issues in debriefing, I prefer to focus on the challenges in learning from failure more than the learning from success, mainly because it better exposes the issues. If you ask a group how they managed to do so well, everyone is very comfortable in telling you how brilliant they were. However, if we need to ask why they performed so poorly, this is a slightly more complicated uncomfortable conversation, so let's talk about that one. I certainly don't mean to frame debriefing as a negative experience; you can learn as much from success as failure. However, if you are able to learn from failure, then you will probably have no problems with learning from success. The reality is that it is the ability to identify, and work at, the weak areas that will drive performance.

A quick health warning

I should perhaps offer some disclosure myself here, and point out that this approach does have a caveat that you should be careful to manage. I would like to think that I am reasonably objective, I have a bit of a perfectionist streak in me, and am definitely somebody who tends to focus on areas for improvement. These are all traits that serve one quite well on the Red Arrows, but they do carry some baggage.

I remember one show at Biggin Hill near London where the weather was terrible. There was low cloud over the airfield and the wind was about 20kts, making for turbulent, bumpy conditions. You can tell from the pilots' voices on the radio how the show is going (in this case, not well), and for the junior guys, who always feel more exposed and are more likely to be the source of errors, there was an acceptance that it was probably going to be an 'interesting' debrief. Sure enough, the prediction was true, and after everybody giving each other a hard time for half an hour, I went out to get some fresh air.

Outside, one of the crowd recognized the red flying suit and came over to me to tell me that he had seen the Red Arrows perform every year at Biggin Hill for 20 years, and that this had been the best show he had ever seen. This illustrated a strange dichotomy: over 99 per cent of the crowd, the people who the show was for, probably thought that it was great. And yet the team had just spent half an hour beating each other up over a 'bad' show. So who was right? Well, both. The show had indeed looked great from the ground. However, the reason that it's as good as it is, is because the team is relentless in its pursuit of perfection, and is measuring itself against a much higher bar than anybody else is holding it to. The downside is that there is probably not enough celebration of success. If you're constantly driving for the next level, in particular in an environment where there is no absolute measure of success, don't forget to pat yourselves on the back sometimes, when actually you are doing pretty well.

I also had a personal illustration of this dichotomy. For a year I employed a woman in Mission Excellence who was in transition between working at a senior level in global pharmaceutical company, and working for herself. At the end of that year, it was a great opportunity for me to get some independent feedback from an experienced business person on the relative strengths and weaknesses of Mission Excellence. She only really made one point: that I was wholly gap-focused – only interested in what could have been done better. She said that this was what made the company successful. However, the downside was that when she came in from closing a big client engagement, she would sense that I treated that as the minimum acceptable standard (true!). She pointed out that it might encourage her to tell her that she had done a great job and give her some positive recognition.

I am wholly bought into the power of debriefing. Just don't forget to celebrate success, and remember that not everybody might be quite as obsessive in the drive for improvement!

Actor/observer bias

Most people, sometime in their lives, stumble across the truth. And most jump up, brush themselves off, and hurry about their business as if nothing had happened.

Winston Churchill

Having given you the health warning to apply the process with care, before looking at specific debrief behaviours, it is useful to examine a concept from psychology that explains really well the fundamental challenge in debriefing. The concept is called actor/observer bias. What the theory says is that if you are an external observer of a situation, you tend to be objective. You have no vested interest, are not involved in the organizational politics and don't hang out with everybody at the weekends. So you call it as it is. It's not difficult to see the facts as they are and define accountability. This is the essence of how management consultants make money.

However, if you are an actor within the event, particularly if it didn't go so well, there is a natural tendency to have a subjective perspective not necessarily supported by the facts. We're all human; we intuitively blame the situation, the organization or somebody else. The expenses scandal relating to UK Members of Parliament in 2009[7] provided a nice example of this. One after another, several MPs were outed by the media, only to claim that they had broken no rules and that it was the system that was flawed. Well, the system may not have been perfect but that doesn't mean you have to milk it dry. The test of acceptable behaviour is not peer group acceptance or compliance with an obviously flawed system, but simply looking at yourself in the mirror in the morning and knowing you did the right thing. Unfortunately, actor/observer bias can tend to skew even that perception – a strong moral compass is required.

Calling things for what they really are will not always make you friends, however, what happens in high-performance individuals and teams is that they have an ability to bridge that gap between actor and observer. They are able to self-analyse their own performance with the same brutal honesty as a third-party observer. This is a simple concept but remarkably challenging in practice: to attempt to bring to human performance the same level of evidence-based observation and assessment that one might apply to financial performance. The challenge is that we are dealing with real people who have personalities, egos and vested interests. In the context of the earlier discussion about feedback and debriefing, it is about taking ownership of the feedback in a completely objective manner, even if it's not what you wanted to hear.

By way of example, a construction company failed in its bid to win a contract to build a number of schools. When the team members were asked why, their answer was along the lines that the client simply didn't realize how good their bid was. This was not quite as arrogant as it sounds; the bid submitted transcended far beyond simply constructing schools, to presenting a vision for twenty-first-century school education. However, to blame the client at this point is pretty pointless. The schools would still be built, just by somebody else. The client was happy; the only loser here was the construction company.

The objective observer, instead of blaming the client, would identify that it is only possible to have lost the bid for one of two reasons. Either the bid wasn't as good as they thought, or they were right and the client simply didn't get it. Either way, they need to analyse the problem and own the outcome. In the latter case, the correct course of action would not be to blame the client, but to take the client feedback, and ask what did *we* do that got the client to the place where they didn't see the value of our fantastic vision?

Behaviour in practice

How do we embed this sort of honesty in the debrief? It starts and finishes with the leader. The debrief is a non-hierarchical learning experience, but that doesn't make it a free-for-all debate, a group hug or a big 'love-in'. It is always facilitated, and normally by the leader of the team or project or task. The leader's behaviour is therefore critical and sets the tone for everybody else. One common feature of good leaders in the debrief is that they will lead from the front in admitting their own mistakes. This act of disclosure is enormously powerful. First, it sets the tone. When the senior person, who may also be the most talented or experienced, starts by admitting their own mistakes, it makes it okay for other people to have made mistakes. Contrast that with the opposite scenario; who will admit anything then? This act also illustrates a simple fact of life: the boss can get it wrong. The boss may not know that he or she got it wrong, so other people need to be able to challenge them without fear of retribution. That sort of challenge and the acceptance of it are strengths, not weaknesses. This is how errors are addressed and performance is improved.

In order to achieve this, we debrief without seniority. Everybody is equal; everybody is there to learn. This may come as a shock to the 'old hands', but the leader can learn as much as anybody else. The great insight can come from the youngest, least experienced person. It's almost more likely to come from the person who hasn't being doing things the same old way for the last ten years. But that person's opinion needs to be treated with respect and given the same weight as anybody else's.

This idea of conveying feedback to the leader is not a chance to give the leader a hard time. However, the leader's performance is a fundamental piece of the performance jigsaw and who better to comment on it than those being led? I have had senior leaders speak to me about this concept and explain that they understand the point and can see the potential value but would not be very comfortable about receiving feedback on their performance in front of the rest of the team. I think it's important to highlight the honesty and self-awareness in that comment. However, my response is along the lines of, 'What do you think the talk is about when you leave the room? You're the only person who doesn't know they all think you messed up. Wouldn't it be better to know that now?'

Let me offer an example. Imagine leading a project on which you are not the most senior person and having to call other more senior people to account for their mistakes. In debriefs in military aviation, this happens every day. Do you recall the discussion of flexible leadership? The person who leads is the person best equipped to lead, not necessarily the most senior.

Put yourself in that situation. Could you challenge somebody upwards like that? Or maybe a better question, if you are already a leader in some context, is whether the people who work with and for you can challenge you like that. Everyone always likes to think that the answer is 'yes', but what is the reality? How would you handle that with someone less experienced than you and junior to you, who hasn't been with the company very long and challenges you on something that has been your little pet project or process? For the vast majority of us, the answer is that we get defensive.

How do you think that more senior officers in a fighter pilot mission debrief tend to behave? In general, the answer will be with humility. They tend to understand how important it is for their own credibility, to be judged to the same standard as everybody else in front of everyone else. And because of that, and this is the whole point, they *learn*. Because of the debrief, there is a learning outcome. This is critical. The debrief is a not a free lunch. It is never about blaming, but the learning must be accompanied by accountability. Almost by definition, if things went badly, then *somebody* needs to change something next time. We try to avoid accountability smearing whereby everybody feels that the debrief was useful, but nobody is actually committed to doing some specific thing better next time.

To keep the debrief objective, we also try to keep it impersonal, using callsigns rather than names where possible. This probably sounds a bit nerdy (and it probably is); however, what we are doing in effect is referring to each other by job title rather than name. It was not Justin Hughes who made all those mistakes, it was some bloke called Red 9. We're still mates in the pub afterwards … sometimes! When you've got nine left-brained testosterone-fuelled males (to date, there has been only one female Red Arrow pilot[8]) who all have an opinion on everything, it can get a little fraught occasionally . . .

And the final bit of the jigsaw is to remember the symbolic effect of your own behaviour. This is ever more important, the more senior you are. Remember when you were starting out, how you would react to, and interpret, the words and reactions of more senior people? As you become more senior, it's important to remember that. Sarcasm, a public put-down, a little joke at a subordinate's expense, or even just rolling the eyes or shaking the head can all have a disproportionate impact on the 'target'.

What we are talking about is keeping communication on the adult-adult level. This will often break down; it certainly happened to me when I was flying. I remember on the Red Arrows somebody more experienced than me making a point about my performance in the debrief. The way in which the point was put across was sarcastic and humiliating; everyone had a good laugh at my expense. Have you ever been there? How do people react to that sort of situation? You may nod and try not to overreact but internally, the shutters are up. You are thinking something not very positive about that person!

There is a great deal of research on communication styles and effective communication. Something like only 15 per cent of live communication is via words (witness the success of the silent movie *The Artist* in 2012), 35 per cent is by voice and some 50 per cent is by body language. This logic applies exactly to my situation in the Red Arrows debrief. I could almost certainly have learnt something from the 15 per cent; however, 85 per cent, the delivery of the feedback, was all wrong and I was no longer listening.

Running the debrief

The biggest challenge in debriefing (apart from finding the time!) is almost certainly addressing the behavioural issues described. But even a great team with respect for each other, the discipline to listen to each other and the ability to be objective about performance, may still not have a great debrief. The next challenge is to structure the debrief. The most obvious danger with the team I just described is that in their efforts to be polite and respectful to each other, they will skirt around the issues, and voice lots of opinions, but fail to really identify the root causes of the performance weaknesses. If you ask ten people their opinions, what you get at the end of it is ten opinions. It may well be that none of those opinions are actually the correct root causes of success or failure that we need to identify for next time. So we need some structure or process to organize the debrief. At Mission Excellence, we model debriefing using the LEARN model:

L Lead by example
E Establish the parameters
A Analyse the execution
R Review the learning
N Notify the learning

Lead by example

As I pointed out, the quality of the debrief starts and finishes with the leader. The leader needs to step up to the plate, set the professional standard and the tone for the debrief. This starts with the same issues which we described for the briefing. Be prepared and ready to start on time.

The leader also sets the behavioural tone. In our workshops, we use a video of the Red Arrows debriefing in which the first thing that happens is that the leader starts off by admitting to a safety infringement that he made that day. This sends out a very powerful subliminal message: it's OK to have made mistakes. It is the leader's task to establish a comfort level and objectivity that turns 'learn not blame but with accountability' into a reality.

Although debriefing is a team game, the role of the leader in the debrief (by inference, the leader of the project or mission, whether the most senior or not) is pivotal, since they are the ones who will set the direction and drill into the issues or not. I always think that debriefing is one of those things that is not too hard to do adequately, but is extremely difficult to do well. It requires some subtle combination of the intellect to ask the right questions and zone in on the right issues, but with the people and facilitation skills to do so in a way that doesn't alienate people.

Debriefing is a difficult thing to 'manage upwards'. If you're leading the debrief, it starts with you.

Establish the parameters

We want to have a debrief, rather than a chat. To make that more likely, it is essential to establish some parameters at the start of the debrief, especially if the attendees are not used to the process. 'Rules of engagement' help to set an expectation for everybody. An introduction might be along the lines of:

'Welcome everybody. We are here today to debrief our performance over the last quarter. To that end, we have an hour and I would like to spend about 15 minutes on each main business area before summing up. We have quite a few people in the room, so please put your hand up and come through me; I will try and capture all the inputs. If there are disagreements, I will let the issue go back and forth a couple of times, but will act as the final arbiter if needs be. Remember that we are here to learn, so please respect your colleagues, but also be honest and direct. If you think that somebody should have done something differently, please so say, but also explain why. Sound reasonable? Ok, let's get underway.'

Straight away here, the leader has set a professional tone and standard which will influence everybody else. He or she has also defined a basic flow for the meeting and set some ground rules for the conduct of the meeting. This is not just going to be a big 'group hug' which goes around in circles and achieves precisely nothing.

Analyse the execution

This is the main part of the actual debrief. And the concept is simple – we just unwind the plan-brief-execute sequence. The flow might look something like this:

Aim
Admin issues

Plan
Brief
Execution

We start by re-establishing the reason we are all sat there – the aim. The anchor point for the whole conversation is whether we achieved the desired outcome. That is what we are measuring ourselves against. You would think that this element is simple and straightforward, but it is amazing how often you can ask people what the aim was and whether it was achieved, and get an ambiguous or unjustified 'yes', when it clearly wasn't achieved as originally defined. If the aim was clearly defined at the planning stage, then it should be possible to state unambiguously whether it was achieved or not. And we need to be objective about that. It is possible that the outcome is not known at the start of the debrief but, where it is, this is what we debrief against. So I start the debrief by firmly re-establishing the aim at the front of everybody's minds.

Next, we get any administrative issues out of the way – things that were ancillary to the mission. It should be possible to cover anything under this heading fairly quickly; don't get bogged down in extraneous detail.

The first major item is the review of the plan. With the benefit of hindsight, was this a good plan? Every item up until 'execution' should be covered fairly quickly, unless it is now apparent that there were some fundamental flaws in the original plan.

The brief is the second item. This tends to be primarily feedback for the leader on their communication of the plan. Having reviewed the plan, did everybody understand that this was in fact the plan? Is there any feedback on the communication style/method?

The main part of the debrief is the analysis of execution. What went well and why? What went badly and why? Why, why, why? 'Why?' is the killer question that will uncover the root causes of success and failure. You may be familiar with the 'Five-why rule': ask somebody 'why' once and you will get an excuse. Ask five times and you will get the true cause. You should note that this needs to be handled with some empathy; it's not an interrogation. The difference between the first answer and the root cause may be quite significant. I once did some work with a car rally team; in a rally, the driver went off the road on the first corner. The engineers' perspective on the root cause was that the driver 'screwed up'. However, a little probing revealed that the driver had flown from South America to Europe the previous night and was exhausted. The reason for this was PR commitments. And the reason for this was, in turn, car sales in South America. So the issue to be addressed was probably not simply 'find a better driver' but to better balance the competing priorities of race team performance versus sales support.

The way to work through the execution is simply to reconstruct what actually happened in chronological order, measuring against the two key questions of what went well/badly and why. Key decision points should reviewed and learning outcomes should be captured as they arise. If possible, it may be helpful to group learning outcomes under a few different headings.

Review the learning

At the conclusion of the debrief, the leader should review the main learning outcomes, with accountability where appropriate (note to self: don't forget to praise the positives). If it was a big project and there were a lot of points that came up, there's no pretending that 50 are going to be addressed immediately. Just concentrate on the two or three most important issues, put them right, and worry about the rest once the big ones are addressed.

Notify the learning

The points that come up in the debrief are only known to those who attended, and many points will be specific to that team or to individuals. But what if points come up that are highly relevant to other teams in the organization? How inefficient is it to let another team go through the same painful learning process that you have just been through? This inefficiency is often most prevalent in sales organizations, where teams are organized in an internal competition by geography or function, and are more bothered about beating another region than any competitors outside the organization. Remember that you get what you reward. The motivational reasons for this are clear, but you are not incentivising any form of behaviour towards the collective common good. And you are definitely going to let the other team go through the same painful learning curve. Even organizations with less focus on internal competition rarely manage knowledge well across the organization. This subject is dealt with at the end of this chapter.

Implementation – when and what

You could read this chapter, understand the concept, like it, but be unsure about how to implement debriefing, or worse, start trying to apply the concept to everything. Here are a few quick tips for application:

1. Debrief things that were time-bounded and had an outcome. It's difficult for me to be too prescriptive but open-ended work where the quality or outcome is difficult to measure will be difficult to debrief. If necessary, try and impose artificial bounds. Break a project into sensible chunks, preferably ones which have a measurable outcome.
2. Only bother debriefing things where there is a return on the investment – that is, you're going to do something similar again and so it would be useful to identify the learning. Interestingly, the only display of the year which the Red Arrows do not debrief is the last one. That particular team will never display together as a team again, so there's no point. (In point of fact, old habits die hard and it's not unusual to find a few of the team having a sneaky look at the video at some point). Avoid having debriefs for the sake of it. They will end up as a short-lived management fad and you will miss a great opportunity to accelerate the learning curve.
3. Debrief against the aim and against the plan.
4. Read the next section on knowledge management.

Knowledge management

Debriefing is knowledge capture. To only capture the knowledge for the benefit of those who attended the debrief is only to scratch the surface of the potential benefits. However, if debriefing is uncommon, then high quality knowledge management systems are rare in the extreme.

The benefit is obvious so I have just dived straight into the practicalities with some examples below.

The key to knowledge management is the existence of a knowledge database in a known location and easily useable format. This needs to be constantly updated from two main sources, external sources of data accessed via research, and learning from experience that can be captured in debriefs. The knowledge database then provides a single source of information for those taking on new tasks, projects or clients. They might access the database either actively, asking for information, or passively, whereby the 'owner' of the database disseminates information to those likely to benefit from it. An example of the process is shown in Figure 6.2.

Let's look at some practical examples. On the Red Arrows, in any one year, it is the same team working together on the same task again and again. The database is a combination of personal learning that exists in people's own heads and the team's standard operating procedures (SOPs). The source of knowledge is learning capture via debriefs. No further dissemination is required.

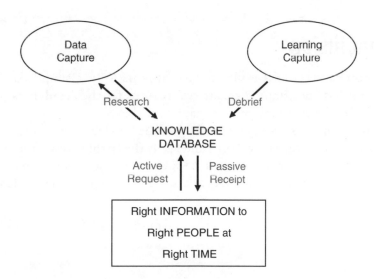

Figure 6.2 Knowledge management system

For a fighter mission, the database is again SOPs plus background intelligence information. The sources are debriefing and research. Access is active. When planning a big mission, I know where the information is and can go looking for it.

For flight safety, the knowledge database is effectively the central safety department. It is informed by debriefing of adverse events, and by data capture, for example, from black boxes. Dissemination is often passive. When the safety department identifies information that operators should know, they send it out unsolicited.

There are a few key points that make this sort of system work:

- The system must be designed by operators, owned by operators and used by operators. This is not something that can be outsourced to some sort of 'knowledge manager'; they will not have the insight or the operational credibility to be effective.
- Credible robust systems are required which capture information from all available sources.
- Access should be easy and information overload avoided.
- The underlying concepts should be kept simple.

Conclusion

In this chapter, I have explored what appears to be a simple concept in some level of detail. There are two reasons for the detail. First, this might be the most important chapter in this book. It doesn't really matter what the status quo or start point is for your team or organization. If you can learn in real time and apply the learning faster than others, you are on an inevitable path to success. The second reason is that it is more difficult than it looks and so I have dissected the challenges at some length.

Get this right and anything is possible. On the Red Arrows, debriefing was the single biggest driver of performance.

Summary of key points

- A debrief is an objective assessment of team performance against a plan, carried out by the team themselves, ideally at the end of a time-bounded period of activity with a defined outcome
- Assessment, an inquiry and feedback are all subtly different
- Actor/observer bias – the ability to bring external objectivity to internal performance
- Debrief behaviour: everybody is equal; everybody is there to learn
- Debrief process:
  - Lead by example
  - Establish some parameters
  - Analyse the execution
  - Review the learning
  - Notify the learning
- Knowledge management: right information to the right people at the right time

Other issues

Bringing others on the journey (Leadership)

What is leadership?

With the above advertisement Ernest Shackleton initiated a sequence of events which would come to define him in history. Shackleton was born in Ireland in 1874, qualified as a master mariner, was involved in four Antarctic expeditions and was knighted for his endeavours. His most famous quest was, having been beaten to the South Pole by Amundsen, his attempt to cross Antarctica overland by foot, from one side to the other. The expedition never got as far as disembarking for the overland section, after his ship, *Endurance*, became trapped in the ice and was destroyed. This set the scene for an epic battle for survival, which presented challenges probably far greater than his original mission.

Shackleton's men were selected through his now famous advertisement. Described as a man of towering ambition and boundless optimism, it is a measure of his personal standing that some 5,000 men applied. In an era long before television and the internet, 5,000 men volunteered to be led by Shackleton on an expedition for which they had almost no detail other than that safe return was doubtful. What does this say about the man?

Before coming back to that question, I need to admit something. Up to this point, I have been guilty of a lack of precision in my writing, which many others are also guilty of, but which now needs to be addressed in this chapter. This is with respect to the use of the word 'leader(ship)'. The problem is that 'leader' and 'leadership' are used interchangeably in two different contexts. The first is in the context of being a 'senior leader' or on a 'senior leadership team'. I would argue that the key word in both those phrases is senior. It is possible to be senior without being a particularly strong leader.

The second way in which 'leader' is used is in the context of others choosing to follow; this trait can exist at any level of seniority in an organization. Exceptional leaders might be in some of the most junior positions. It's difficult to get away from this ambiguity since the dual use is so deeply embedded in common usage. However, in order to be precise about our meaning, for this chapter at least, we are focused on the latter interpretation of 'leader' in its more literal sense.

As a general rule, and notwithstanding any specific subject matter expertise required, the core competencies for general management tend to be relatively agnostic to sector. Successful general managers will be characterized by strength of ethical character, professional competence and intellect. We find it helpful to break out those three different aspects using the model that I introduced in Chapter 2 and repeated in Figure 7.1.

Our development of this model was significantly influenced by Dr Stephen Bungay, although the thinking is not unique to the military, Bungay or Mission Excellence; the basics are empirically derived common sense. First, a quick reminder of the core concepts in the model:

1. Direction is the ability to set and articulate clear direction, to provide vision or, more accurately, 'intent'. This might be referred to as doing the right thing. This is predominantly an intellectual activity predicated on critical and creative thinking, and communication skills, and becomes more relevant in more senior roles.
2. Leadership is the ability to bring others with you on the journey, such that they *choose* to follow of their own free will (otherwise it is seniority, not leadership). This is predominantly a moral and emotional

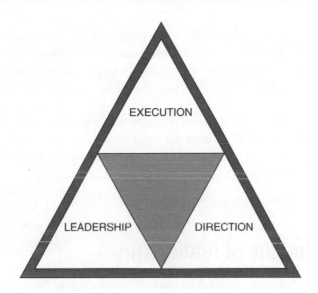

Figure 7.1 The hierarchy of organizational performance

   activity based on one's values and behaviours and is valid at all levels
   of an organization.
3. Execution is the ability to deliver results and get things done – what
   might be referred to as doing things right. This is a physical activity – something happens as a result; it is a function of people, clarity
   in task and roles, planning, management of time and resources, and
   learning for continual improvement.

Despite the imprecision in the way in which the word 'leader' is often
used, I believe that many would intuitively still agree with the above
description. Certainly, if you ask people what qualities they would asso-
ciate with a great leader, invariably the vast majority of the responses
are value-based, and have little or nothing to do with seniority, intellect
or management.

I have no intention of trying to define leadership any more than as in
the preceding framework. Many so-called definitions exist, none of
them actually definitive, and everybody has an opinion, from the Boy
Scouts to Harvard Business School, in addition to just about anybody
who has been sufficiently senior and high-profile to have been asked

for their thoughts on leadership. My plan is to keep it simple, and the starting points are that it's about engaging, motivating, and inspiring, and it's value-based. For me, you couldn't really sum up the essence of leadership any better than Slim's quote below:

> *Officers are there to lead. You will neither eat, nor drink, nor sleep, nor smoke, nor even sit down until you have personally seen that your men have done those things. If you will do this for them, they will follow you to the end of the world.*
>
> Field Marshal Bill Slim

Descriptions of leadership

For those who are interested in other definitions and opinions, in lieu of putting my own head above the parapet, I have provided a selection here:

> *Our chief want is someone who will inspire us to be what we know we could be.*
>
> Ralph Waldo Emerson

> *Leadership is lifting a person's vision to higher sights, the raising of a person's performance to a higher standard, the building of a personality beyond its normal limitations.*
>
> Peter Drucker

> *Leadership is what causes people to give their last ounce to achieve something without counting the cost to themselves; it's what makes them feel they are part of something greater than themselves.*
>
> Field Marshall Bill Slim

> *Leadership is the art of getting someone else to do something you want done because he/she wants to do it.*
>
> Dwight D. Eisenhower

> *Leadership is getting people from where they are now to where they have not been.*
>
> Henry Kissinger

Before you are a leader, success is all about growing yourself. When you become a leader, success is all about growing others.

Jack Welch

The growth and development of people is the highest calling of leadership.

Harvey S. Firestone

The task of leadership is not to put greatness into people, but to elicit it, for the greatness is there already.

John Buchan

The great leaders are like the best conductors – they reach beyond the notes to find the magic in the players.

Blaine Lee

There are many elements to a campaign. Leadership is number one. Everything else is number two.

Bertolt Brecht

Are we happy with the general idea? There's not much mention of intellect, management, task or resources; this is a people game.

The dichotomy of leadership

While the model in Figure 7.1 considers the overlap of three different competencies desirable in a senior executive without prioritizing, it should be noted that in practical terms, execution and leadership are not necessarily equally weighted.

The management of time, task, people and resources is your basic critical building block in delivering outcomes. Leadership is how you do it in a way in which people are engaged (i.e. amplifies performance and makes it sustainable). The important point to note here is that while we would like to have great leadership and engagement, what you are measured on is management and execution – the ability to deliver outcomes. And while it is important that the strategy (direction) is broadly sensible, the reality is that poor execution is a far bigger and more common stumbling block.

To understand the practical implication of this asymmetry more clearly, I refer to my experience of asking people what traits they would want in a great boss for whom they would like to work. The responses are invariably value-based – for example, loyalty, integrity, respect, consistency, trust, courage and so on – all of which are broadly consistent with the story that comes out of the previous quotations. We want our boss to be a great *leader* and that means strong (positive!) values and behaviours. Consider now what our boss's boss wants, as shown in Figure 7.2.

What do you want from the person who works for you? Well, you might want a good working relationship and to see consistency between his/her behaviour and the organizational values. However, more than anything, what we want from the person who works for us is often to make our own life easier, to get the job done without requiring constant support and intervention. In the final reckoning, what our boss's boss wants is results. It takes a rare long-term perspective, strong conviction and high emotional intelligence to place behaviours on an equal footing with results.

This is the dichotomy of leadership. People and organizations want great leaders, but the reality is that you can go an awfully long way in an organization, maybe right to the very top, on intellect and

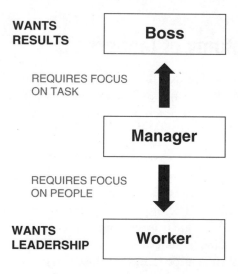

Figure 7.2 A simple organization

results – those are the things that get you promoted. You are highly unlikely to achieve a senior executive position without execution skills, but you could achieve it without strong leadership ability. And the corollary is definitely true; being a senior executive does not mean that a person is a good leader. Churchill grappled with this issue for much of the Second World War, finding that many of his most senior officers, who had been promoted to that level in peacetime, were found to lack the ability to inspire and the will to win when their leadership competency was illuminated in the particularly harsh spotlight of total war.[1]

I saw a psychologist present recently on a closely related issue to this argument about the relative importance of leadership and management competencies. The argument was framed around the case that emotional intelligence (EQ)[2] is more important than IQ (Intelligence Quotient is a test score that is the 'traditional' measure of intellectual or logical capability), a line of thinking that originated in Daniel Goleman's highly successful book, *Emotional Intelligence*.[3] While this makes a nice angle for those positioning themselves as EQ experts, for me it fails the common sense test. Management (execution) is the basic building block. A great manager will survive long enough to work on their leadership skills, but no matter how strong your values and people skills, without some reasonable competence in management and execution, you may not be around long enough to show off your leadership. Note that I am not arguing for a second that high EQ cannot have an exponential impact on performance. It's the icing on the management cake, transforming the cake from ordinary to exceptional. However, although a cake without icing can still be acceptable, icing with no cake is a victory of style over substance.

Much of this book to date has been about the cake. In this chapter, I want to put some focus on the icing, on the difference between competent task-focused manager and the exceptional leader.

The Shackleton story

There are any number of potential subjects for leadership case studies, although the field narrows somewhat when leadership is considered as described earlier. In practice, business as usual tends to expose intellectual and delivery abilities. Leadership ability would almost always improve team or organizational performance, but could be considered (highly) desirable rather than essential – as just mentioned – you can do very well with strong management and merely adequate (or worse) leadership.

The priorities start to change though, when you are asking people to scale new heights or to take on or do things that they don't want to, and maybe don't even consider possible. This is when the ability to motivate and engage moves from highly desirable to essential; the ability to lead becomes the critical success factor. And leadership is about values and emotional intelligence. These are things that may not be routinely exposed during business as usual (unless they are really bad); core values and behaviours are often only exposed by some form of trigger or stress. Examples might include the need for courage (whether physical or moral), balancing risks and benefits, placing the needs of others above your own, and making short-term sacrifice for long-term good.

With that in mind, some of the best leadership examples come from situations where the leader and the team or organization are working under real stress, where people's degree of commitment to the cause, or their acceptance of challenges that might appear beyond their perceived abilities or limits, is highly influenced by their belief in a person and what they really stand for. Back to Shackleton ...

Journey to the ice

Of the 5,000 respondents to his advertisement, Shackleton chose twenty-eight men. Other than building a team with a specific set of skills, Shackleton placed a heavy emphasis in interviews on what would now be called 'cultural fit' and camaraderie – he wanted team players who could work together. It may not be a coincidence that the Red Arrows employ similar thinking to this day.

Shackleton's ship, *Endurance*, departed Plymouth on 8 August 1914. It sailed to Argentina and then on to South Georgia in the South Atlantic. Another twenty-eight men went on a separate vessel, *Aurora*, to the opposite side of Antarctica to build a camp and set out supply bases for the inbound trekkers. On 5 December 1914, the last link with civilization was broken when *Endurance* set off from South Georgia; there would be no communication outside of the expedition until 20 May 1916. The original aim was to cross the icecap on foot during the southern hemisphere summer of 1914/15; however, from the outset, the backup plan was to wait until 1915/16 if necessary. As it turned out, the 1914/15 period was a particularly bad year for ice and by 19 January 1915, *Endurance* was frozen in.

The significance of ice versus land here may not be obvious to all readers. While Antarctica is covered in snow and ice, it is a fixed land mass, like any other continent. However, there is also an ice pack which extends in the winter and breaks up in the spring and summer. The ice pack itself drifts on the surface of the sea and is subject to constant reshaping by nature's forces; *Endurance* was trapped within the ice pack, at a considerable distance from its planned landing point.

On 27 January 1915, the decision was made to put out the fires of the ship's boilers and engines to preserve coal, and on 24 February the ship's normal routine effectively ceased. *Endurance* became a hotel locked solidly in the ice until the spring. On 1 May 1915, the sun set there for the last time for the winter (there were, in fact, two more further brief sunrises due to an atmospheric anomaly) and the crew spent seventy days with minimal natural light in the polar winter. Temperatures dropped to –30C and lower, and 70mph (112kph) winds piled at least 100 tonnes of snow against the side of the ship, while the noise of the ice floes pressuring against each other was a constant reminder of the danger below.

If Shackleton was disappointed at the sequence of events, he failed to show it. He kept the crew busy with tasks that were shared equally, as well as sport and games on the ice and regular entertainment evenings. Shackleton had a non-hierarchical approach to routine tasks and led by example, taking his turn in the daily activities including scrubbing decks, finding inspiration in camaraderie and promoting strength through unity. He would invariably lead by example when difficult or unpleasant chores needed to be done. He also engaged in a highly participative leadership style, exercising authority when required, but routinely including crew members in decision-making and deferring to his subject matter experts. As spring arrived, it was hoped that the ice would break up and release *Endurance*, however the huge pressure generated by the breaking of the ice and movement of the giant ice floes posed a clear danger of splitting the ship's hull.

Abandoning ship

On 27 October 1915, Shackleton conferred with the ship's captain, made the difficult decision to choose camping on the ice over the relative warmth and protection of Endurance, and gave the order to abandon ship. When a ticket lottery had to be held to determine who got sleeping bags and who just got a blanket, Shackleton characteristically took the first blanket. On 21 November, *Endurance* finally slipped below the ice. Shackleton had a great ability to deal in current facts – what had happened had happened. He did not dwell on the past, but focused on his new mission: to save every life. Described by one of his men as the greatest living optimist, he retained their unshakeable confidence.

Shackleton and his men initially made camp on an ice floe. Based on assessment of movement, the initial plan was to allow the ice floe's natural drift to take them towards Paulet Island, some 250mi (400km) away, where Shackleton knew of a station hut with supplies, which was occasionally visited by whalers. They tried sledging for a few days, pulling *Endurance*'s lifeboats with them, but made almost no progress and eventually set up a more permanent base (Patience Camp) on an ice floe, with no option but to submit to the mercy of the winds and the currents. Their direction of movement passed close to Paulet Island but it was inaccessible to them.

Eventually, after around five months on the ice floe, the ice started to break up and the crew put to sea in three lifeboats. The primary aim was just to make landfall. Shackleton elected to make course for Deception Island (200mi / 320 km away), but it quickly became apparent that their food would not last at such a slow rate of progress. Hope Bay (80mi / 130km away) was considered as an alternative; however, after four days when the weather cleared enough for a navigation check, it was found that they had moved 30mi (48km) in the wrong direction. Shackleton knew that the crew was deteriorating fast in the open water, and the priority became simply short-term survival. When the closer Elephant Island was spotted, he took that option. The crew had spent seven days in lifeboats on the open sea, 170 days on ice floes, and it had been 497 days since they were last on dry land. While they celebrated a return to terra firma, Shackleton's challenge was only just beginning.

Sea survival

Elephant Island was a long way from any shipping routes and was not used by whalers. Despite the opportunity to build a land-based camp and catch fresh meat again, there was no realistic hope of any rescue (why would anybody even look for them there?), and Shackleton immediately ordered one of the lifeboats be prepared for a crossing to South Georgia. This was 800mi (1280km) in a lifeboat, navigating only by the sun and stars, which were rarely visible, across some of the roughest seas on earth. A navigation error of 0.5 degrees would mean that they would be lost at sea. On one level, this was madness. At another level, however, given the prevailing tides and winds, it was the only manned post that they might realistically reach in an unpowered boat, so for Shackleton there was no other option.

Once again, Shackleton combined his optimism with some realism about the situation. Anecdotal evidence indicates that he took two of the more difficult crew with him so as not to upset the dynamic of those he left behind. He also only took four weeks' worth of supplies, working on the principle that any more was a waste. They would have found land by then or be lost at sea. His instructions were that if he didn't return, the remaining men, under his second in command, Frank Wild, should take to the sea again for Deception Island.

In the lifeboat, three would be 'on deck' at any one time and three in the tiny 5ft x 7ft (2m x 1.5m) waterlogged cabin pretending that they could sleep. Everything was soaking wet, not least their clothing which hadn't been changed for seven months. Their sleeping bags shed their hair and became bald, while the men's skin chafed and became raw. Although progress was reasonable – 60–70mi (96–112km) per day – gales and storms brought near-zero temperatures, and there was a constant effort to chip away at the ice that formed. The ice became such a problem that all excess weight was ditched overboard, including two of the sleeping bags.

After a week, a sunny day made possible the first navigation check in days – it was determined that they were over halfway to South Georgia.

A few days of unremarkable progress followed before the worst storm of the crossing. Clearly, there is no reason why Shackleton would have been in any better shape than anybody else. However, he continued to lead from the front, insisting on a mouthful of hot drink for everybody as soon as he detected worsening symptoms of cold in anyone. On the fourteenth day, parched with swollen tongues, the men sighted land but had to spend another treacherous night at sea in a storm before finally making it aground on South Georgia.

Land survival

Unfortunately, the storm had taken its toll on the lifeboat and it would not be possible to sail it further around to the whaling station at Stromness. The only option was to cross South Georgia's uncharted 10,000ft (3,000m) peaks on foot for 17mi (27km). Two of the men were too weak to make the journey, so Shackleton left one to care for them and set out with the other two. To put this in context, three experienced professional climbers with all the latest equipment recently took three days to complete a re-creation of this journey. Shackleton and his two companions, having just survived an incredible sea crossing, completed it in thirty-six hours.

Even during this trek, Shackleton remained acutely aware of their situation; he refused to let the group sleep, due to the risk of never waking again. They reached the whaling station on 20 May 1916 and, after rescuing the other party of three by boat, set sail from South Georgia aboard a Norwegian whaling vessel. However, Elephant Island was inaccessible due to ice (of course!) and it eventually took another three recovery attempts and three months to rescue the main party on 30 August; they had survived 105 days, and not a single life had been lost. Shackleton then immediately devoted himself to the recovery of the crew of his second ship *Aurora*. Of the men, twenty-five out of twenty-eight were rescued alive.

Lessons

Shackleton clearly combined many strengths and of course more than a few weaknesses, and there is no small element of physical courage and stamina in this story. However, in the context of this chapter, what was it that Shackleton brought to the party that inspired 5,000 men to volunteer, and held *Endurance*'s crew together through one of history's most incredible survival experiences?

Shackleton was undoubtedly a visionary and optimist. He always projected confidence and utmost belief, building optimism and confidence in others, while keeping his inner worries to himself, his diary and a small group of close confidants. However, his optimism was not a naïve pipe dream but was based on reality; he simultaneously dealt with the hard facts of a situation head on, never shirking difficult decisions and taking significant risks when the situation called for it.

Shackleton inspired respect by leading by example, never asking people to do things which he would not do himself. In fact, his behaviour was quite the opposite. He combined humility with awareness of the symbolic significance of his own behaviour and took his turn doing the dirty work. There was a consistency of standards in what he expected from himself and from others. He was genuinely concerned for the welfare of his men and put their needs above his own. And he included others in the decision-making process; this both tapped into all the expertise among the crew and helped to build a real sense of ownership and commitment.

It's true that not many of us will be tested in the way that Shackleton was, but there are still some powerful lessons that translate across to most environments. I would argue that much of leadership is situational, and what worked for one person in one situation might not work for somebody else in a different situation. If it wasn't for the Second World War, Churchill would be remembered as no more than a moderately high-profile politician in the early part of the last century. However, when it comes to engendering commitment, motivation and inspiration, many of the underlying values are relatively timeless so now I would like to put some more relevant context around a few typical core values.

Values into action

I am of the opinion that in many walks of life, explicitly including the commercial world, it is possible to go a very long way, maybe even right to the top of an organization, without your values being deeply tested, as long as you don't do anything too bad on the behavioural front, and you are delivering results. The same is even true of the military, in particular in peacetime.

In the peacetime military, to reach the very top, you need the intellect for command, the management ability to oversee execution and probably the political awareness to survive. I have seen senior officers with fundamentally weak leadership. You might expect that, in wartime, the prioritization of results would be even greater. However, the thing with wartime is that results are not achieved by management alone. When you are asking people to give everything of themselves, and possibly to make the ultimate sacrifice, the strength and quality of leadership will almost always be the decisive factor in determining success or failure.

It should be self-evident that it is other people's perception that will determine whether you are a leader or not. You cannot decide that you are a leader or be promoted into leadership. You are a leader if other people follow you of their own free will. People form an opinion of you as a person and as a leader, not by what you believe, or by what you say, but by what you do. People at work don't know if you are a committed member of your local community, or if you are very worried about how to best handle thorny personnel issues, or if you give a percentage of your income to charitable causes (although if these things are true, the values which drive them may well exhibit themselves in other ways). They don't know what's going in your head. They can only make a judgment based on the evidence presented to them by what you do and which is visible to them. So it's not your values that are the critical issue here. And it's certainly not the values you claim to stand for. It's the way in which your true values are exhibited through your behaviour. Let's take a look at what some core values might look like in action.

Respect

I always think that in the context of leadership, respect is almost the master value. If you respect somebody, then you are probably prepared to listen to them and, within their field of competence, to be led by them (if they're not engaging or motivating you, they are simply managing you; you are unlikely to go the extra mile just because of them). Other values, and the behaviours through which they are demonstrated, tend to build or destroy respect. Now respect, in practice, is a bit like trust. You don't choose to respect somebody or not; you just do. So what behaviours build respect? Perhaps a more useful approach is to turn that question around and ask how do we show somebody respect?

Imagine that you work in a big office and you are quite senior, and every day you walk in and see the security guards at their desk. There are always lots of other people around and people greeting you. How would you show respect to the security guard? One easy answer is to say 'Hello' – to take a few seconds out from your day to acknowledge and greet him. Or what about 'Hello John' – you've actually made the effort to remember his name. Or what about 'Hello John, is your wife better now' – not only have you taken the time to engage with him, but you are actively listening in the moment when you stop and talk; you remember exactly your previous conversation about his wife being unwell.

It is easy to underestimate the impact of the leader's behaviour in this context. It may not seem that big a deal to the 'big cheese' heading up to the office in the C-suite. But that is to overlook how much importance the big cheese attached to the symbolism of senior executives' behaviour when she was starting out as the office junior. This is the 'shadow of the leader.' Small positive gestures from senior executives can have a disproportionate impact. One word of warning though: you need to buy into this and be authentic to make it work. Saying anything is probably better than saying than nothing; however, leadership by numbers and pretending to be somebody's best friend will soon be exposed for what it is.

I saw an interesting example of this issue about names, respect and spending time talking to people while on the Red Arrows. We had a new leader join the team during my tenure and with a fairly long handover period, he had time to immerse himself fully in the whole organization. He chose to spend some of the handover time working on the flight line with the engineers, including getting his hands dirty doing some of the messier, less popular tasks. By way of full disclosure, I should point out that the pilots had mixed opinions on this – it was slightly odd to be walking out to the aircraft with your future boss working on the flight line building personal relationships with the groundcrew before the current boss had even left. The incoming boss had no doubts about the value though. It gave him an insight into the practical issues facing the engineers, which was invaluable. Added to which, he learnt all the engineers' names (around 100). You should not underestimate the impact and symbolism of that one action in terms of building relationships and credibility.

I have seen other equally effective variations. An executive in banking with whom I did some work used to place great store in replying to all his emails personally, even when he was in senior roles. He has now reached a level (and volume of email) where this is simply no longer practical, but it was with some reluctance that he started to share the load and he still deals with a surprising number of difficult issues personally. The same manager was responsible for taking over an underperforming business with offices all around the country. So he decided to get to see the problem first hand. Each Monday, he boarded a train with a small backpack, no PA or staff, and set off alone around the country with a Blackberry and a notebook. I am not pretending that there were no other factors at play, but that business was remarkably improved in less than a year.

Even today I notice small behaviours in this context. A client, who is CEO of a major financial services institution, still responds to emails from me personally, while a couple of personal associates who have hectic professional schedules tend to organize any meetings through their PAs. Efficient practice and good use of limited time or just rude? You decide . . .

For a final comment on respect, I return to the old favourite of punctuality. If you are chairing a meeting of ten people and you start 15 minutes late, what message that does that send? It may say something about professional standards, but it says something rather deeper about the relative importance you attach to your time compared to your attendees' time. Finishing late is almost worse. People are busy; they have other meetings to go to. If you overrun, you are essentially saying that you are more important than their next meeting. Whether that is true or not, it's not a great message to send if you want to earn their respect. People form an opinion of you based on the behaviour they observe.

Loyalty

Let's say that your boss comes up with a plan of action with which you disagree and think is a poor use of resources that is unlikely to achieve anything significant. You go back to him and argue the issue. Your boss listens to your opinion, discusses the issue in more depth, and then decides to politely ignore you. The new plan is then briefed to you and the other direct reports, asking you to brief it on in turn to your own teams. Do you:

1. Just brief it with no further explanation?
2. Brief it with a strong positive endorsement giving some extra local context and explaining how great this will be?
3. Brief it with apologies and a: 'sorry about this, but the boss says . . .'?

This is quite a subjective scenario, but has a right answer in my opinion. You may guess that my 'right' answer is (2). Loyalty is a two-way street and you owe your boss the same loyalty that you want from your own team. If they had issues, you would want them to talk internally to you and not to betray you or 'do your team's dirty washing in public'. If a decision on a course of action were required, and not all of the team agreed with your decision, you'd ask them to unite behind it and give it their all anyway. That is exactly what your boss is asking of you.

Now it has been put to me that if you feel strongly that you are being asked to endorse something with which you fundamentally disagree, then answer (2) would actually be betraying your own integrity. Intellectually I understand that argument, but don't agree that it should take you to a different conclusion. There is a bigger picture here about alignment, respect and loyalty. Once you start to undermine those issues, your execution challenges will significantly multiply. If you really feel that strongly, challenge up beyond your boss (having exhausted all other options, and informed your boss that you plan to refer upwards), ask to be moved or resign. Just don't take the backstabbing route.

Values under pressure and ambiguity

I started this chapter by reflecting on what leadership is, arguing that it's about people choosing to follow you. I then made a case that the reason people make that choice is because of the values you hold, and that the way in which they can see your values is through the behaviours you exhibit. However, the preceding examples are 'low hanging fruit'. We can all choose to exhibit great behaviours under low stress and when there is little or no cost to us as a result of those behaviours. What people are really made of is often only visible under stress or ambiguity. In those circumstances, we start to sort the leadership wheat from the chaff.

Ethical dilemmas

Consider the following examples. For each one, just reflect for 10 seconds on what you would actually do. Not what you'd like to do or what the 'right' answer is, but what you would do? What have you done when faced with similar situations in the past?

1. You are a man and you are walking along a quiet street late at night, and you see a woman being physically threatened on the opposite side of the street by a guy who is clearly bigger and stronger than you; what do you do?
2. You became aware of something within your organization which is fundamentally wrong, but to expose it might have significant personal costs (promotion prospects, even loss of job); what do you do?

Both scenarios will cause stress, but the 'right' answer may be less obvious than first appears; there may be all sorts of complicating factors. You may think you saw a knife in the first example. Is it better to face the threat and risk both being seriously injured, or to run and call the police, who might not arrive in time? I have intervened in a not too threatening version of the first scenario only to find out that it was a domestic argument and have the woman turn on me, encouraging the man to 'sort me out.' Thanks . . .

The second scenario might carry downsides other than just the risk to your career. Other innocent or not so innocent bystanders may be dragged down with you. Your organization's reputation might be permanently damaged. Think about a situation where you become aware of something in your own organization that is 'not right'. This can vary from the downright illegal (e.g. fraud) to the marginal (e.g. a misleading sales pitch to an unsophisticated buyer) or from simply bad judgment to a conflict of interests (e.g. senior manager writing promotion reports on somebody with whom they are involved in a secret relationship). Attempting to address any one of these issues directly is unlikely to make you many friends, and there may be different approaches to achieving the same outcome, some of which are lower profile. Turning a blind eye to something illegal though, even at the lower end of the spectrum of seriousness, is the start of a very slippery slope.

I had an interesting example of a moral dilemma in a rather different context during my RAF career. Another pilot confided in me about some significant stresses in his personal life, which for various reasons he was unwilling to share with his boss. As a result of the issues, by his own admission, his head was all over the place and he was barely sleeping at night. His primary aim in talking to me seemed to me to be just that – to talk to somebody. The only caveat he placed on me was confidentiality.

However, having given that freely, once I understood the situation, it turned out to be a commitment that might be difficult to honour. Clearly my main concern was to do the right thing by him and be there to support him. And he had asked me to respect his confidence. But there was also the small matter of this individual flying a £25mn fighter plane on no sleep and with his mind focused elsewhere. The potential existed for him to do untold damage to himself and others. I decided to go back and explain my dilemma to him. He needed to remove himself from flying and if he didn't do it himself, then I had a moral obligation to highlight his unfitness to fly. The way I framed it was 'What would you do if somebody approached you like this?' Fortunately common sense prevailed; he took himself off flying and we remained friends.

Leadership dilemmas

The common factor in the two examples I started with here is that the situation or facts were relatively clear. Notwithstanding my previous comments, the 'right' path is also relatively clear. Let's make it more difficult still by layering in some ambiguity:

1. You are the MD (boss) of a nuclear site with a speed limit of 10mph (16kph) and on your very first morning at work, you see somebody speeding; what do you do?
2. You are the director of a professional sports team who has staked his credibility on drug-free success and find that one of your team has been associated with drugs, not on your watch, but many years previously; what do you do?
3. You have strong evidence that one of your reports has deliberately flouted organizational safety rules, but your trusted deputy assures you that this was not the case; what do you do?

We could talk about these examples at length and in a group of upstanding people who would consider themselves to have strong values, some will have the opposite opinion to others. So how do you reach a decision? In these scenarios it helps to have some reference points or frameworks to view the issue from different perspectives.

Philosophical frameworks

Philosophy provides some useful start points as to approaches (my own interpretations):

- Utilitarian. What is the solution that serves the greater good? The cracking of the Enigma code in the Second World War provides a perfect example.[4] Some intelligence could not be acted on for fear of showing that the code had been cracked. As a result innocent people died. Imagine having to make that decision . . .
- Justice. Is there a legal right or wrong? Has the law been broken? Are you prepared to countenance that, or must the law always be followed? We have an interesting example in the United Kingdom where it is illegal to assist in euthanasia. However, a small number of people have made the decision to support a loved one with a terminal condition in ending their own life, in particular at one clinic in Switzerland. Nobody has yet been prosecuted (at the time of writing), but they are breaking the law, potentially with serious consequences for the assistant . . .

- Right. What is the 'right' thing to do for the individual(s)? What would you want to happen if the situation was reversed? US President Obama believed that it was the right thing to do to work towards closing the detention facility at Guantanamo Bay. While both the utilitarian and justice issues are ambiguous, Obama's primary concern appeared simply to do what was right.

Viewing a scenario from different frames of reference will not necessarily lead you to a definitive answer but it will introduce some objective criteria into your decision-making.

In terms of leadership, how you handle the thorny, subjective, difficult stuff is likely to define you in other people's eyes. People form an opinion as to what you really stand for, and whether they want to follow you, not by what you think or say but by what you do. And what you do in the sorts of situations just mentioned will ultimately define what you stand for. Making difficult decisions will not always make you too many friends, but the ability to make those decisions is what you are getting paid for. There's nothing wrong with being a popular leader, but it's not a popularity contest. And you tend to find that if you make a decision for the right reason, and communicate the reason, then people will respect you for having the courage to do the right thing, and will come on the journey with you, even if it's a harder path.

What happened?

For the record, the three scenarios above were all real. What happened in practice (these are the abridged versions):

1. The MD decided to take a low-profile route and gave the speeder an informal warning off the record. However, he subsequently found out that the speeder was verbally abusing him as 'weak' and the 'same as all the others', and fired him (there was bit more to the HR/legal side of this, but those are the basic facts). I should point out that this was not an ego issue but a measured decision. On reflection, the MD now admits he was probably harsh but does claim that his decision may have achieved more than a two-year road safety campaign would have done.

2. The second example is in the public domain and concerns Sir Dave Brailsford at Team Sky (cycling). Brailsford released the individual in question, for which he received some negative coverage and feedback (the person had done nothing wrong in this role). Brailsford's response was along the lines of, 'if you are putting yourself out there as standing for a certain set of values and way of doing business, then non-compliance must have consequences'.
3. The third scenario is based on an aviation accident, the 1994 crash of a B52 aircraft at Fairchild Air Force Base in the US.[5] The situation described is based on the actual sequence of events, but did not necessarily happen in the quite the simple clear-cut way I framed it in this example. I am not commenting on the outcomes of the actual scenario, merely illustrating a point and encouraging you to think about what position you may have taken.

What works for you

Leadership is values-based, and your ability to lead others is likely to be highly influenced by the impression they form of you based on your behaviour. But what are the *right* behaviours? What about leadership styles? When should I choose a different one? Like a lot of things in life, the answers to these questions are probably both simultaneously simpler and more complicated than might first appear.

By way of example, honesty, integrity and moral courage are related concepts but not necessarily the same. Honesty is at some level, simply telling the truth. To me, integrity is acting in a way that is consistent with your values (doing the right thing when no one's looking was a rather nice way I heard of putting it), while moral courage implies deliberately putting yourself in harm's way (whether physical or otherwise) in defence of what you believe.

What would you do?

For an example of where all three come in to play, consider the senior National Health Service manager (and experienced clinician) earmarked for the top of the organization. During his tenure in a political-level role, it became apparent to him that the root cause of a specific major incident within a hospital had been systemic in nature and that responsibility fell to his own central office. He was clear that the only route available was to go public and take the responsibility at the central office level. In turn, it was made quite clear to him by his political masters that such a route would have serious consequences. He did what he thought right and that was the end of his upwards career trajectory. Did he show integrity and do the right thing, or did he take the moral high ground, thereby denying himself the chance of the top job where he could have had far greater long-term impact on the organizational culture? Or was there a compromise solution available? You decide . . .

To be or to do?

The problem here, and with some of the previous examples, is one of compromise and shades of grey. Colonel John Boyd,[6] a noteworthy strategic thinker originally in the US Air Force in the 1950s and 1960s, had an opinion that in a hierarchical organization like the military, there are essentially two types of people: those who want to *be* somebody, and those who want to *do* something. How he defined those categories was that those who wanted to be somebody wanted to reach the 'top of the greasy pole'; they wanted power, recognition and status. Those who wanted to do something wanted to add real value to the organization. In Boyd's model, these were mutually exclusive aspirations. He thought that, almost by definition, the 'doers' would need to challenge the status quo and rock the boat. This doesn't make you many friends, if you want to get to the top. The 'be' people, on the other hand, will at some point need to make political compromises in order to engage positively with disparate demands and stakeholders, in order to continue their rise.

Was Boyd right? Possibly. Boyd was certainly in the 'do' camp, surrounding himself with like-minded thinkers and, while still having fairly low recognition even now, had an enormous influence on fighter aircraft procurement (for the better, from the operator perspective), and indeed on US military doctrine. The flip side is that he was famously described by one US general as a '24-carat pain in the ass'. We live in an era of globalization, and work in diverse organizations; Boyd was a superb thinker and was enormously influential, but sometimes an out-come can only be achieved through compromise. You need people like Boyd around, but if everybody was like him, the world would be a more difficult place.

Be true to yourself

There is no 'one size fits all' solution here as to what great leadership looks like. What comes out as always true for me, however, is the require-ment to be authentic and to be true to yourself. Not everybody will have liked Boyd but many will have respected him and known what he stood for. It is suggested in this chapter that an important foundation stone of leadership is simply generating respect. This is really not that hard. Be true to yourself. Live your values. Treat others as you would want to be treated. Remember the symbolism of your behaviour. Show a little humility. Lead by example.

Summary of key points

- It is important to be clear what you mean by leadership – it is often confused with seniority
- In its pure form, leadership is the ability to engage, motivate and inspire; it will be driven by values and emotional intelligence
- In most situations, management is essential; leadership is highly desirable, however strong leadership can have a disproportionate impact on performance
- In high-stress situations, leadership becomes the critical success factor
- People form an opinion of you as a person and as a leader, based not on what you say, but on what you do

Chapter 8

Missing sink holes (Risk)

Profits to a business are like breathing is to life: absolutely essential but not the reason for living.

Anon

Author's note: I hope that the general reader will find this chapter interesting and that the principles are widely relevant, but it is written primarily with high-reliability / high-risk industries in mind – for example, energy, aviation and healthcare, and so on. While most, if not all, organizations need to manage risk, in those industries, it is a critical indicator of performance, with dire (often fatal) consequences for failing to do so.

Thinking about risk

I was recently on an aircraft and about to travel from London to Munich. The flight was slightly delayed before leaving the gate due to a technical problem that required the resetting of an onboard computer. When the aircraft finally got on the runway, and shortly after starting to accelerate, the pilot aborted the take-off and the aircraft returned to the gate. It turned out that the problem was not fully resolved and that the engineers would need to do some further work to fix the computer. While at the gate (still on the aircraft), one passenger informed the crew that he wanted to get off with his family and take a later flight. A perfectly reasonable conversation ensued in which the captain came to speak to the man personally but he was insistent that he wanted to get off, which the crew duly arranged. Given that he wanted to travel on a later flight, there is a fairly reasonable assumption that he thought the next aircraft would be safer. My question to you is whether, in fact, he increased or decreased his risk by changing aircraft? We will return to this example in due course.

Introduction

I could write a whole book on decision-making and risk, and many would see it as a separate issue to the rest of this book. However, although it is a specialist area in its own right, it would seem remiss not to include a chapter on risk in a book on execution and excellence. The ability to manage risk is self-evidently a relevant factor. First, a couple of cornerstones:

1. Philosophically, I regard risk and safety as different aspects of the same thing. One could argue that risk is a mitigation issue and safety is an outcome. In practice, however, one tends to hear phrases like risk management and safety management referring to something similar; mostly the difference in the general usage is that safety management is mitigating against injury or accidents to humans, while risk management is about mitigating against other adverse outcomes. Once one moves beyond the realm of personal safety (e.g. correct clothing, low-level compliance, etc.), I would argue that the cultural and non-technical issues overlap significantly. The principle of a bad decision leading to a bad outcome is the same irrespective of whether anyone gets hurt.

2. I do not regard risk management as something which can be addressed independently of operational performance. It is something that is meaningless in isolation; managing risk effectively is a key constraint of *how* we do business and is therefore a performance metric. If safety is literally your number one priority, then don't do anything that carries risk. To paraphrase the quotation at the start of the chapter: 'Risk management is to performance what breathing is to life …'. The problem is that many activities that we might want or need to undertake carry both systemic and idiosyncratic risks, and so we need to be able to manage them. It is important to be clear that as a key (critical) performance indicator, risk management is a 'means' not an 'end'. On a related note, I have heard the head of an oil industry trade body ask: 'Let's not make safety a competitive point of difference.' The sentiment is laudable but unachievable. It assumes that unlimited resources can be devoted to safety. I would wholly support the concept of sharing information and good practice when it comes to risk and safety, but the reality is that

when companies are faced with choices in the allocation of finite resources, and a constant tension between operations, finance and risk, then risk management is not an abstract concept or exercise in compliance. It is a performance factor ultimately owned by operators, and our success in addressing it is directly related to the organizational culture – how we prioritize it against other performance factors and what resources we allocate to it.

Through Mission Excellence, I have had insight into a number of industries where risk management or safety are paramount – for example, healthcare, construction, energy and asset management – and had the opportunity to compare the various approaches to my previous experience in fast-jet aviation. My observation is that many organizations instinctively target 100 per cent systemization of risk issues. I propose that such a purely systematic approach to risk management will only prevent an unplanned or adverse outcome in a finite number of scenarios. In particular, making good decisions faced with ambiguity and imperfect information will require a holistic or cultural approach to risk; you can't systemize the risk out of what you can't model.

Modelling risk

First, consider the predictability of adverse outcomes. If I toss a coin and one side indicates a good outcome, and the other side an adverse event, then all things being equal, I can be confident that for each individual toss, there is a 50 per cent chance of an adverse event. Over hundreds or thousands of coin tosses, the average number of adverse events will converge towards 50 per cent. So the chance of a bad outcome is predictable, and I can capture the risk of an adverse event in a single number. This line of thinking could be applied to any manner of activities that have a discrete number of random outcomes – you can statistically predict them. And if I can model the risk like that, I should be able to manage it.

The same general line of thinking can be applied to more complex scenarios. If you are a manufacturer of high-tech aircraft engines and have lots of experience and data capture technology available to you, and if the engines are being operated at sufficient scale to smooth out statistical anomalies, then it is likely that you can predict average failure rates with some degree of accuracy. In fact, with modern datalink technology it is possible that even when the symptoms of a problem do appear, they can be identified early enough to prevent the problem ever actually occurring; it is even possible for the manufacturer or airline to be aware of a potential in-flight engine problem before the pilots. However, to return to the key point, the combination of experience, technology, high reliability, and a statistical base of thousands or millions of operating cycles allows average failure rates to be predicted with reasonable confidence. You can capture the risk in a model or number and it has meaning. By extension, the risks can be managed or mitigated.

When you're talking about actually operating an aircraft or airline, the number of factors increases exponentially, but the principle still holds. When one thinks about the reality of what happens, it is incredible that commercial flying is so statistically safe. Three hundred people get inside a metal tube weighing 100,000kg, supported by two metal wings which actually bend, and containing thousands of miles of electrical wiring and thousands of tonnes of fuel. The tube flies 7mi above the earth for maybe 5,000mi, at 500mi an hour, getting blown off course by variable 100mph winds, deliberately separated from hundreds of other metal tubes by only 300m, before landing with pinpoint precision on the other side of the world in fog on a piece of concrete 50m wide, having used 95 per cent of its fuel. Now I don't wish to worry nervous fliers, but the fact that you can do this is truly amazing; the fact that it hardly ever goes wrong seems nothing short of a miracle. The combination of minimal risks of equipment failure, together with high quality training (including behavioural – see later), rigorous and systematic application of regulation, standard operating procedures and checklists and so on, allows many of the variables to be isolated and the risks modelled, mitigated and managed. What the airline industry has done very cleverly here is to systemize the vast majority of the risk out of the operation.

Commercial aviation has been regarded as a leader and benchmark for many aspects of teamwork and delivery in high-risk environments. However a paper in the *BMJ*[1] argued that in fact, military aviation provided more relevant lessons for medical teams. Despite the inherent complicated nature of the challenge, operating a commercial aircraft safely from point A to point B can largely be achieved through a *predictive* approach. Airline staff might see this differently, but in terms of safe operations, the task is fairly discrete, well defined and repetitive and many of the variations that might cause problems can be identified and modelled in advance, and captured in processes and decision-making trees.

The limits of the systematic approach

However, if you are performing open-heart surgery, flying a fighter jet, drilling for oil or investing in stock markets, you start with a plan, but the only certainty you have is that it will never work out as planned. The execution of the task is highly *reactive* to things that happen along the way. And given the number of risk factors, many of which may not have been identified at the outset, few of which are discrete, and almost all of which might be correlated in ways which are not immediately obvious, it is clearly impossible to model all the risks or to systemize the risk out.

It is still vital and important to put the necessary risk systems and processes in place, but they will be insufficient as soon as a situation is encountered for which there is no rule. This is slightly disappointing because, in extreme adverse events, that is the time when you really want people to get it right, and it is the time when limits of a purely mechanistic approach are likely to be most exposed. I am not suggesting for a second that systemized process and contingency planning are not important. As the CEO of a FTSE-100 engineering business put it to me: 'You earn the right to deviate from standard operating procedures (SOPs)'. But the problem remains that one major completely unforeseen catastrophe can kill more people or destroy more shareholder value than ten years of incremental gains in processes and contingency planning.

It is impossible to eliminate randomness, bad luck or the inherently unpredictable. However, rather than accepting that and building the capability and resilience to cope, it seems that some managers and organizations prefer the illusion of systematic control (a mantra actually used by one company). In fluid, reactive environments, which are subject to complex unpredictable cumulative risks that are near impossible to model or mitigate with any process-driven or linear technique, how does one approach the issue of risk management?

The beginning of a solution

The approach to risk in fast-jet aviation is to take a holistic perspective and to employ safety processes and models as just one part of a *culture of safety*. The idea is that one can't possibly build a process for every scenario (although you should make a good attempt at the more obvious scenarios), so rather than attempting to give people a full set of solutions, the organization provides a set of rules, guiding principles and default procedures, together with both functional and behavioural training, and empowers people to make decisions to deal with the unique situations they end up facing.

As part of that same culture, there is a heavy emphasis on those leadership values and behaviours (e.g. courage, integrity, objectivity) that support open, honest, evidence-based, decision-making, independent of hierarchy, with *safety as the single overriding constraint*. It's the difference between giving a man a fish and teaching him how to fish. In this case, it's not possible to provide all the solutions, so the aim is to equip fighter pilots with the ability to reach safe solutions themselves. For fighter pilots, safety or risk management is not simply an exercise in compliance, or something which is outsourced to a separate department; it's owned by the operators. Safety is what they do. If it can't be done safely, or at least within agreed acceptable boundaries of risk, then it can't be done at all.

Risk management and operational excellence enjoy a symbiotic relationship. Managing risk is a key performance indicator of operational excellence, while safety is not an end in its own right but a natural by-product of the pursuit of operational excellence. So everything in this book to date about the pursuit of high performance is relevant to this chapter. The difference is that the risk/safety key performance indicator is of overwhelming importance in high-risk and/or high-reliability environments, which means that certain other factors, all of which are relevant to some extent in most high-performance environments, assume far greater significance.

The remainder of this chapter proposes some constituents of a safety culture based on my experience as a military pilot and then compares that experience to other high-reliability environments. I split out the constituent parts of a safety or risk management culture into five factors:

First the *systematic mitigation of risk* through a foundation of

- organizational issues, and
- procedural issues.

Followed by the building of a wider *safety culture* by addressing

- operational excellence,
- behavioural issues, and
- leadership.

Flying to Munich . . .

Before dissecting each of the above in some more detail, what about the passenger jumping ship from our flight to Munich? I have asked a few people whether they thought he had increased or decreased his risk; on average, more thought the risk had decreased. There is a known issue with the current aircraft that wasn't fixed the first time. Therefore, why stay on it?

The problem I have with that thinking is that it's linear, assumes that this is a closed system in which all the variables are known, and contains a number of untested assumptions. It might be worth considering some or all of the following:

- No pilot ever takes off in an aircraft which they think has a problem which might cause a crash. It's always unknown unknowns or at least unanticipated combinations of circumstances that cause a crash. It would be deeply irrational for it to be any other way.
- The engineers are now highly focused on this aircraft and a named individual will have to personally sign that it has been fixed. Most aircraft never get this level of engineering focus before departure.
- There are lots of moving parts on an aircraft and we are focused on a single data point. There is an assumption that the second aircraft has nothing wrong with it, with no actual evidence to justify that.
- The pilots of this aircraft had shown themselves to be conservative in their approach to safety. Aborting a take-off in a commercial aircraft is a big deal, especially for what appears to be a relatively minor fault. I have total confidence in these two individuals.

I'm not sure that we can reach any definitive conclusion on the decision of the passenger, but I would argue against any opinion that he has reduced his risk. In my opinion, for all of the reasons described, he is more likely to have increased it. What is clear though is that he has made an emotional, rather than a rational decision. It's impossible to reach a conclusion through logic alone. When dealing with a complex system, the approach to risk has to be holistic and cognizant of the fact that you can't exert 100 per cent systematic control. The solution is always going to be cultural. First, the lessons from military aviation . . .

Organizational issues

Organizational issues in this context refer to the way in which basic good practice is embedded through regulation, supervision, training and assessment.

Regardless of the heavy emphasis on empowerment and individual responsibility in this book, there is still a clear requirement to mitigate the most obvious risk factors through rules and regulations, for example, low flying rules, minimum separation distances and so on. These are limits for which there is almost never any rational argument to operate beyond them without an unacceptable reduction in safety margins. Regulation might be seen as the minimum requirement for safe operations set by an external supervisory body; compliance is mandatory.

In addition to individual compliance with regulation, mutual and cross-supervision is an accepted part of operating fast-jet aircraft. While authorizing and supervisory powers are delegated to suitably able and experienced individuals, it is common for the designated supervisor not to be necessarily the most senior line manager, and they would be wholly within their powers and responsibilities to challenge up the command chain. Indeed all aircrew, no matter how junior, are encouraged to challenge any practice that they regard as unsafe or carrying undue risk.

Safety- (or risk-) related training is another consistent theme throughout a pilot's career. The most regular example of this is in the frequency of simulation training. Simulation is actually used in some very different contexts, starting with the acquisition of core functional skills and processes, where the requirement is for high fidelity. This form of training requires accurate replication of equipment and environment to be as realistic as possible. However, for competent operators, the next level is to exercise decision-making. Such scenario-based simulation can be completed using much lower fidelity. The scenario needs to be credible, more so than equipment (this might be simply a desktop exercise). The power of this training is the ability to simulate high-risk scenarios in low-risk environments; crews are permitted to learn from mistakes without operational consequences.

Both implicit and explicit within the training mandate is an element of assessment. What is unusual about this when compared to some other environments is that the assessment is agnostic with respect to rank or seniority. To provide some context, a squadron commander, who is the senior line manager, will each year be required to undergo a review of core flying skill and, separately, of instrument flying ability. And these tests will normally be carried out by a subordinate (who is a specialist in training and assessment) on the commander's own squadron. Every two years, the commander's and her squadron's tactical ability will be assessed by a separate specialist assessment unit. This concept of routine internal audit, including by junior members of one's own unit may seem alien to many, especially when compared to, for example, consultant doctors who until recently were subject to intensive assessment during training until around age thirty-five, and then no further formal assessment for the rest of their career. How arrogant would it be for a squadron commander to fly around in a £35mn aircraft close to human and technical performance limits, with the potential for a mistake to cause untold damage and loss of life, and yet to assume that they were above ever having their core competency revalidated by virtue of seniority?

Now one might assume that this combination of rules, training, supervision and cross-checking stinks of micromanagement and overregulation, but the reality is somewhat different. The aim of routine ongoing assessment is not to catch people out, but simply a chance to check that no bad habits have crept in and to give people a few pointers, as well of course as a chance to apply some more proactive performance management for those with significant weaknesses or unsafe habits. And because professional standards, ability and safety are such an integral part of the whole operation, many pilots will regard training rides and assessments as a chance to demonstrate their prowess, rather than feeling checked up on. There is a chance to build confidence and positively impact on career prospects.

A strong organizational approach to compliance with regulation, training, assessment and internal challenge to poor practice or non-compliance is the first building block in a systematic approach to risk management. The rules set the boundaries within which the subjective decision-making takes place.

Procedural issues

Procedural issues in flying operations most often refer to standard operating procedures (SOPs), exactly the same concept as discussed in Chapter 4 on building capability in the team. SOPs allow the systematic application of best practice and define a consistent modus operandi which is the default way of operating in the absence of any specific brief to the contrary.

There is widespread use of SOPs within the military, although this does not make for an inflexible rule-bound organization. In fact, it's quite the opposite: extensive use of SOPs means that operators do not 'reinvent the wheel' for every mission. All the basic procedures for operations and coordination of different units are standardized, which releases a lot of spare mental capacity for dealing with any unique aspects of the task. This has advantages over and above the blindingly obvious:

- It introduces predictability into operations. Predictability massively reduces the training burden and gives enormous flexibility. It is possible to chop and change elements or individuals within the team without any impact on performance or increased risk; everybody is already 'working from the same sheet'. Remember that SOPs are not rules. If a situation requires divergence from SOPs, that is fine as long as it is planned and briefed in advance, and everybody is aware of the non-standard elements. However, in the absence of any brief to the contrary, the default procedure is predefined.

- It systemizes best practice. SOPs are not a haphazard collection of procedures; they are the assimilation of hard-won corporate learning over many years, which continue to evolve over time.

SOPs are less rigid than rules; they will not be perfect for every situation, but they should define a robust, effective and safe default mode of operations for a majority of situations.

Operational excellence

Much of the relevant material with respect to operational excellence has already been covered. Here I only summarize how the factors combine to support safety. When a fighter pilot is facing a situation where a constant stream of decisions is required in a high-risk environment, characterized by ambiguity and an overload of imperfect information (sound familiar?), he has the advantages of:

- A set of rules to keep him out of the most obvious dangers.
- Mutual support and cross-supervision from other experienced team members, operating in a near flat hierarchy.
- Honing of his core functional skills set through regular training, assessment and feedback.
- Corporate collective experience of many years captured in SOPs, defining some default options.
- Behavioural training to increase awareness of his communication style and the impact of that on decision-making and team performance.
- Scenario modelling covered in the simulator or in mission-specific contingency planning.
- Proactive learning from all his previous debriefs, both the ones he led, and the ones where he had the benefit of other people's learning, including senior leaders.
- A deeply ingrained approach, both organizationally and individually, to a margin of safety.

Behavioural issues

On 27 March 1977, two Boeing 747 aircraft collided on the runway at Los Rodeos Airport in Tenerife. The crash was the deadliest single accident in aviation history and 583 people died. What marked this accident out, apart from the tragic loss of life, was that there were no significant technical failings on either aircraft or within the airport system. The accident was wholly due to human, organizational and environmental factors. Before this point, the effect of human behavioural dynamics on performance had been the preserve of NASA. After this point, it was embraced by the aviation industry, both civil and military and the rather poorly named Crew Resource Management (CRM) was born, part of what is known more widely known as 'Human Factors'.

While accident rates have reduced markedly since 1977, it is still the case that the ability to mitigate human factor risks still lags significantly behind the ability to mitigate technical or process risks. In fact, in aviation, the relative contributions have reversed. Boeing estimates[2] that in the early days of flight 80 per cent of accidents were caused by the machine and 20 per cent by human error. Today, around 80 per cent of accidents are attributed to human error in some form, and only 20 per cent to machine or equipment failures.

The CRM big six

The development of CRM over the last 30 years is a reflection of the growing importance attached to human communication and decision-making in resolving safety-critical issues. The 'big six' factors driving effective CRM are generally agreed as:[3]

- Communication – engaging in a participative leadership style and exhibiting behaviours that encourage open honest dialogue and challenge. Experience in the commercial airlines shows that the most effective crews spend approximately 30 per cent of their time communicating, even in high-stress scenarios.[4]
- Choosing behaviour – selecting a behaviour that is appropriate to the situation or role. A simple example would be that if you are the leader, to step up and accept the decision-making responsibility which goes

with the role; however, if you are not the leader, behave like a team player in support of the leader, while letting the leader lead.

- Feedback – giving and receiving feedback is the subject of a wealth of literature and training, and the concept and key issues are no different in this context; they are closely related to communication issues.
- Situational awareness – the ability of an individual to build and update a mental model for the world in which they are operating; it implies an ability to understand the practical impact of their decisions on other external players and the impact of other's actions on oneself.
- Medical factors – human performance is highly susceptible to variations in well-being and in physical and mental fitness. Again there is a vast amount of literature in the various professional fields. However, it is hopefully self-evident, for example, that alcohol and fatigue impair performance. More subtly, in high-risk environments, it is important to recognize that factors such as bereavement and divorce are significant inducers of personal stress in yourself and colleagues, and have considerable potential to impair decision-making.
- Decision-making – this is, of course, 'what it says on the tin'. While good communication practice tends to imply a participative leadership style, decisions still need to be made and acted upon. Sometimes any decision is better than no decision. However, remember that changing a decision does not necessarily mean indecision.

CRM training is formally mandated for commercial airlines and in military aviation. Its importance is clear recognition that no matter how much technology and automation improves, for the foreseeable future the necessary but weak link is likely to remain the 'man in the loop'. The latter brings enormous cognitive ability and perhaps more importantly can apply judgement, intuition and experience to subjective and/ or ambiguous situations. However, he or she also brings finite processing capacity, ego, personality, group think (the tendency of groups to veer towards harmony or conformity in their thinking) and so on. More than anything, CRM is about developing some self-awareness of these weaknesses and improving awareness of the impact of one's own behaviour – in particular, the implications of that for performance and safety.

Behavioural issues are almost by definition subjective; changing behaviour is a long-term commitment, and compliance and ability are not easy to measure empirically. However, the extensive experience of the commercial aviation sector has clearly demonstrated a tangible improvement in performance and risk management through behavioural training.

Leadership

The difference between success and failure often rests on the strength of a single quality: leadership.

Winston Churchill

In one sense, everything I have written is ultimately about leadership. Only the senior leaders will initiate the rules, processes, procedures and training to make any of the above happen. However, defining a set of processes will no more influence activity than writing values like 'teamwork' and 'trust' on a mission statement in the company's reception area and expecting them to influence organizational behaviour. Whether consciously or unconsciously, people respond to what gets measured, rewarded and recognized. If you talk a good story on team and values, but pay individual bonuses based on performance, what sort of team behaviour do you expect? If you sell the importance of risk management, but reward only returns, what will be the organization's attitude be to risk? The CEO of a newspaper may have been unaware of the specifics of phone-hacking, but when an organization's culture is to get the big story, no matter what it takes, the leader cannot subsequently deny accountability for what happens within that culture.

Imposing a set of safety rules is easy; building a culture of safety is hard. Executive sponsorship is not about talking; it is about walking the talk. The courage and integrity to deal with difficult issues and accept responsibility for failures need to be combined with the objectivity to make true evidence-based decisions.

We have seen numerous organizations where the senior leadership team is genuinely united on an issue – for example, that there is a no-blame culture. However, when you ask line managers about the barriers to open honest communication within the organization, they instantly refer to the blaming behaviours of senior management (by the way, it is no good the senior leadership team claiming that 'the workers' have got it all wrong; perception is fact here). Nobody will put their head above the parapet if they think that there is a pretty good chance of the messenger being shot. More than anything, what we are talking about here is the symbolic effect of your leadership. Nothing has changed from the previous chapter on leadership. People form an opinion of you as a person and a leader not by what you say or what you communicate, but by what you do; not the values you claim to hold, but the way that your values are exposed through the behaviours which you exhibit.

Safety leadership in practice

A wonderful example of the impact of strong principled leadership in a safety-critical environment is provided by the story of Paul O'Neill at Alcoa (the primary source for this story was Charles' Duhigg's *The Power of Habit*[5]). In 1987, he was a surprise and relatively unknown choice as CEO and investors eagerly awaited his first presentation to hear his plans for the business. The bigger surprise was that the opening and main theme of his presentation was all about worker safety. His focus on that as the main key indicator of how the company was performing more generally went down like a lead balloon with analysts and investors. O'Neill was no fool and knew how to run a business, but he clearly understood the relationship between safety and operational performance, laid out the safety message on day one and most important of all, resolutely stuck to it. O'Neill's safety initiatives reduced Alcoa's accident rate from one per week to a situation where some facilities would last several years without losing time due to accidents. It is no coincidence that in the same period, he transformed business performance. During O'Neill's tenure (he retired in 2000), a million dollars invested on day one would have generated another million dollars in dividends and increased in value fivefold.

The Royal Air Force has not been without its challenges on this front. Some years ago, there was a perception building on the front-line that, in the absence of definitive evidence to the contrary, there was a tendency to blame aircrew error for accidents. This becomes most contentious in the case of a fatality, where both decency and process dictated that blame should not be apportioned to the deceased unless no doubt existed (my phrasing). Of course, once you lose the confidence of the line managers and operators, it is a big challenge to get it back, and a healthier culture was only restored after some very public commitments and long-term effort by a new head of the organization.

With the right leadership behaviour at the top, however, you start to create an organization where leadership can exist at every level. Empowerment, devolved decision-making and responsibility can only thrive in an environment of mutual support and trust, where individuals have confidence that if, when faced with a difficult situation, they make a reasonable decision for the right reason, they will be supported in the case of a genuine error of judgement or where their decision is undone by operating hazards. If you're doing something that is implicitly difficult and dangerous, it does carry risks and it won't always work out perfectly. If you have done everything you can to protect your margin of safety, and act with the highest professional standards, then no one can ask more than that. Sometimes it just goes wrong. Rather than blaming people, we try to use this as a learning opportunity for everybody.

In addition to the leadership attributes already mentioned, one should never underestimate the value and importance of common sense in making risk decisions. It's kind of an extreme form of objectivity, trying to drill to the heart of an issue by cutting through the noise to really zero in on the underlying logic, often by asking the most basic 'dumb-ass' questions. In his book, *Supreme Command*,[6] Elliot Cohen forms an extremely positive impression (contrary to some commentators) of Churchill's ability to exercise high-level command, by asking the simplest and yet most probing and penetrating questions of his military leaders. Cohen refers to this as 'massive common sense.' In a world of complexity and information overload, do not underestimate the value of massive common sense against which to benchmark decisions and thought processes. Fitzroy Maclean offers a wonderful personal insight into Churchill's style of thinking in this context in his book *Eastern Approaches*.[7] When he told Churchill of his concern over increased support for Tito and the post-war risk of communism, Churchill replied along the lines of: 'Out of the resistance in Yugoslavia, is he killing the most Germans? ... Good, give him all the help you can.'

Only leadership will bridge the gap between aspirations, commitments, plans and outcomes. Without consistency, symbolism, alignment of reward and recognition, and core values such as integrity and objectivity, as well as massive common sense, a culture of safety or risk will remain a pipedream.

Other industries

The challenge in applying some of the concepts just outlined is that they are partly counter-intuitive – less systematic control, not more, and they fly in the face of the desire of organizations operating in high-risk environments to be seen to have processes in place for every possible scenario. However, forward-thinking organizations do recognize the inherent risks in 'over-systemization'. I recently saw a senior executive from a major oil company present on this issue. He noted that the organization would like (for lots of good reasons) to automate every aspect of rig operations it could. His problem was that during a four-year 24/7 operating cycle, lots of things happen that have not been specifically predicted. And the more you automate the operation, the less well equipped (and empowered) operators are for the one time when you need them to apply judgment.

With that in mind, I turn my attention to some observations of other industries. I would emphasize that this is not a subject that lends itself to watertight conclusions, and the comments which follow include, by their very nature, some broad generalizations. However, I have had an unusual opportunity over the last thirteen years to gain a broad perspective as to the approaches in other sectors, and have seen some best-in-class thinking and solutions to which I was never exposed to as a pilot. I have also had the opportunity to observe the relevance and degree of penetration of the more holistic approach that I advocate here.

All of the sectors considered, namely healthcare, asset management, petrochemical and construction, are subject to extensive regulation, either directly or indirectly. However, there are marked differences in their application of procedure, behavioural training, approach to operational excellence and leadership.

Healthcare, in particular emergency care and operating teams, has perhaps the greatest synergy with aviation: cross-functional teams that change every day, working in situations where communication and decision-making routinely have the potential to carry life or death consequences. Much has been made of the common ground with commercial aviation, and many CRM-type programmes have been introduced. However, I would agree with the *BMJ* writer who argued that the greater commonality actually exists with military aviation due to the highly reactive nature of the task, which is often inherently unpredictable, and it is therefore impossible to model, mitigate, or systemize out many of the risks in advance.

Asset management probably has the least obvious common ground with aviation, and offers perhaps the greatest contrast in the general approach to risk management. Risk in this world is not generally connected with injury or death but the chance of an investment reducing in value or failing to meet a particular target. The underlying decision-making challenge is remarkably similar, however, even if the approach is not.

Construction and petrochemicals are grouped together, since I find that there is a high degree of homogeneity in their workforce demographics. I highlighted the key factors previously in Chapter 6 on learning: technical industries and male-dominated workforces in slightly macho cultures. The same cultural issues relevant to learning apply more widely to safety.

In the following section I have summarized observations against each of the factors.

Organizational issues

Healthcare: Historically in the UK NHS, organizational factors have probably not been optimal for building a safety culture. At the macro level, the NHS is huge, without any one team responsible for setting the organization's direction and culture. Teaching hospitals, individual NHS Trusts, Royal Colleges and the Department of Health will all pull in various directions and with different agendas. And let's not forget that this is an organization of over 1 million people; the leadership challenge is immense.

At the micro level, doctors have high standing, both within healthcare and in society generally, and do a job requiring high intellect and a lot of specialist knowledge. This leads to a danger of the 'hero doctor'; teams often are led by a single consultant, and there is little cross-supervision or upwards challenge. While there is a system for accruing professional development points, this does not always imply meeting any training standard; until recently, there was no formal requirement for any further professional assessment once consultant level was reached. However, there have been significant positive steps in recent years, with training in team behavioural skills becoming ever more embedded, including advanced courses utilizing simulation of actual clinical scenarios, and the implementation of continuous professional development.

Asset Management: Even more than healthcare or aviation, asset management is enormously affected by the cult of the hero. Star managers are publicly feted and rewarded beyond their wildest dreams. While large organizations have sophisticated risk management and governance processes in place, the star culture does not naturally lend itself to cross-supervision and upward challenge. There is heavy reliance on modelling, but although this is in one sense a form of simulation, it is not used to test the humans in the decision-making process in the same sense as simulation in aviation and medicine.

Construction and Petrochemical: These industries have made remarkable progress in recent years, in improving individual and collective attitudes to health and safety. Although there is some resistance to supervision, it is very much the norm and while re-validation of core competency is a newer initiative, a heavy emphasis is placed on training and qualifications.

Procedural issues

Healthcare: The benefits of standardized process are clearly visible in the taking up of initiatives such as the WHO surgical safety checklist

(Chapter 5B). There can be resistance to the implementation of SOPs and checklists, with people arguing that you need a more flexible approach in dynamic environments. However, experience in aviation shows that standardized processes do not make you inflexible; they are what make you flexible; they eliminate mistakes in basic or safety-critical processes while simultaneously 'freeing up your brainpower for the difficult stuff'.

Asset Management: I have limited personal insight into the use of SOPs in asset management, although predefined actions in the event of drawdowns, market movements and liquidity limits are generally designed with the intention of mitigating risk and could be argued to be a form of SOP.

Construction and Petrochemical: Clear overt executive sponsorship of safety is common, together with wide implementation of rules, processes and procedures. So is there even an issue to discuss? Well, I would argue that the procedural approach to risk may have actually gone too far in some companies in these sectors. There has been blanket application of health and safety rules to every aspect of companies' operations, which shows significant commitment. As an example, I have spoken at many conferences for oil and gas companies and have more than once been warned about the protocol for holding the handrail when stepping up to or down from the stage. However, is this overt executive sponsorship and consistent application of best practice? Or is it compliance for its own sake? And does it actually improve safety? What are the statistics for lost work days due to injuries while mounting the stage at conferences? Is the risk the same for walking down three steps from a stage as for walking down a metal-grilled staircase on a North Sea oil rig in a force eight gale?

If the focus is solely on compliance, then the danger is that, taken to an extreme, you start to remove any responsibility for individual decision-making and compliance wins over common sense and leadership; in fact compliance becomes the end rather than a means to an end. Personally, I think that it is a good thing to be forced to 'load a different programme' when in the higher-risk environment. On military airbases, there is a whole different set of rules in force when you are in an aircraft operating area as compared to the headquarters 100m away. You actually walk across a red line that defines a different environment, and warning signs remind you that new rules apply. While I am a strong proponent of 'how you do the little things is how you do the big things', and the impact of leadership role modelling, I am less than convinced about the impact of office safety, handling coffee cups and how to navigate a staircase on operational safety; I fear that the opposite may be true.

There is clearly an essential place for a set of rules and procedures, but it is only one part of the story. Blanket application of rules and procedures runs a clear danger of desensitising individuals to the 'real' risks.

Operational excellence

Healthcare: The WHO checklist, by its very nature, starts to introduce a level of task organization and is the first step in an execution cycle. The other end of the cycle is the debrief process, which has started to get some localized traction through After Action Review (AAR). The difficulty in widespread implementation is resistance to feedback combined with scepticism in terms of the value add, not to mention time pressures. It is easier to show the value of a simple briefing since it instantly brings clarity and organization to the team. The value of AAR is more difficult to demonstrate in the short-term, but there is clear evidence of progress nonetheless.

Asset Management: In my opinion, the most interesting aspect of the asset management industry in this context is how theoretical models are used to inform decision-making. There is nothing whatsoever bad about this in principle, but the practice probably has some limitations. Any number of models are used to calculate risk and produce numerical outputs that supposedly give some indication of the likelihood of losing money. One of the most common is volatility, which in general terms is a measure of the amount by which an asset tends to vary over time from its mean value (time horizon is critical here; if an asset loses short-term value, does it really matter unless you are a forced seller?). Another common term is 'value at risk', which is essentially an indication of what percentile falls within certain probability limits for the size of a future financial loss. These are examples of technology (or theory) informing decision-making. Technology can be very powerful in this context, but we just need to be aware of the different degrees of confidence associated with different data sources, and the requirement for interpretation of information within a wider context.

In aviation, it is implicitly assumed, with good reason, that flight instruments provide perfect information as to the aircraft performance. The problem arises when technology utilising imperfect input data is assumed to produce perfect output data. Volatility and value at risk are relatively straightforward compared to some financial models, but are still theoretical models that rest on all sorts of assumptions.

Asset management seems to be heading in the same direction as commercial aviation in the context of 'systemizing the risk out'. However in commercial aviation, I previously claimed that 'the task is fairly discrete, well defined and repetitive and many of the variations which might cause problems can be identified and modelled in advance'. How much of that holds true in asset management? The individual asset manager operates in an ecosystem where few of the variables are discrete, there are many hidden correlations, and market movements are the result of possibly hundreds of thousands of individuals making decisions, often based on perception, group think and behavioural forecasts as much as they are based on fundamental evidence.

The models are clearly going to contain incorrect and/or unjustifiable assumptions in some situations, which is fine, provided that the limitations are well understood and those weaknesses are factored into the human decision-making. Believing that imperfect synthetically generated risk data are perfect though, is the worst possible scenario – it would be better to have no theory or technology at all. For a pilot, no flight instruments are better than incorrect flight instruments; it is better to simply look outside and use 'raw data' than make decisions based on instruments containing unquantified errors.[8] I would argue that it is impossible to accurately model some of the risks present in asset management, especially in so-called tail events,[9] the once-in-a-lifetime occurrences (or several times in the last few years!) when you need some understanding of the risks most of all.

Rather than placing such reliance on the technical aspects of risk management, perhaps a more holistic approach to risk would include: employing models as just one part of a wider picture including contingency planning; collective decision-making; improved alignment of incentives with both investor time horizons and appetite for risk and reward; strong leadership values and behaviours; and massive amounts of common sense.

Behavioural issues

Healthcare: I don't think that it's unreasonable to say that healthcare has been about 15–20 years behind aviation in the adoption of CRM training and techniques. Aviation also suffered from the 'hero captain' until improved data recording and accident investigation techniques started to expose the myth. In many cases, it was not the technical problem that caused the crash, but poor team effectiveness, communication and decision-making in dealing with the problem. However, without the formal mandating of initial behavioural training plus refresher courses in the NHS, the initial progress made may take a while to really become embedded.

Asset Management: You get the behaviour you train for and you get the behaviour you reward. The low emphasis on personal development, combined with huge individual rewards directly tied to return achieved, have the potential to produce some fairly predictable selfish and narcissistic behaviours. In contrast to aviation, the risk is not owned by the operators; it is owned by investors, with managers often sharing upside benefits but not downside risks. Alignment of reward with calendar targets, which may or may not be relevant to investors, only serves to muddy the waters further. If star fund managers emerge who are objective, disciplined, take a long-term view, and have a genuine deep-seated respect for risk and investors, it may be in spite of and not because of the industry in which they work.

Leadership

The leadership issues are remarkably similar across the sectors, although the NHS probably offers the biggest challenge due to its size and structure. In any high-reliability environment, it is essential that risk and safety are both literally and metaphorically right at the top of senior managers' daily agenda, and that they truly understand the symbolic impact of their personal and behavioural commitment to a genuine no-blame culture. Unless they practice 'overt executive sponsorship, "over-communication", deployment of champions and most importantly, training and reward of the right behaviours' (see Chapter 3), then processes, procedures and initiatives will do no more than scratch the surface.

Conclusion

I do not pretend for a minute that the military offers any panacea solution as to how to build a culture of safety or risk management. It would not be difficult to disprove that theory. However, at the tactical level at least, the inherent dangers of operating fast-jet aircraft in a changing and reactive environment, and the requirement to make important decisions faced with ambiguous imperfect information, have led to the evolution of a more holistic approach to risk than is seen in some environments. Compliance with regulation is mandatory, and with SOPs is normal, but these are simply building blocks. Given that it is impossible to systemize the risk out, greater emphasis is placed on empowered decision-making in accordance with a set of guiding principles, and inculcating a way of thinking about risk, which will give individuals the best chance of getting it right in the moment. Other sectors and organizations have different approaches, some of which are definitely best-in-class. And I would not presume to tell somebody else how to do business. However, it is my aim to challenge assumptions and thinking.

For those sceptics who are concerned about a whole new set of problems that might be generated by empowerment and delegated decision-making authority, I conclude with a heart-warming story from a completely different world. I know a nursery teacher, Jane, who is passionate about the benefits of very young children having the opportunity to 'play in the woods'. She believes that environment offers all sorts of development opportunities not seen in the classroom or traditional play areas. However, she is only part-time and, when she is not there, some of the other teachers are nervous about taking the children to the woods because of the health and safety implications and the increased potential for an accident. Jane's solution is very simple: she gathers the three-year-olds around the play area and asks them to work out the dangers and what rules they need to follow to stay safe. And with a watchful eye she allows them to self-administer and regulate the management of the risks.

Most people respond very positively to being trusted with decision-making authority and desperately don't want to let either the giver of that authority or themselves down. And you can guarantee that when the operators understand and own the risks, and share the downside, they will be pretty focused on a margin of safety. It's common sense, really.

Summary of key points

- Risks in predictable stable environments can be modelled and managed
- It is possible to largely 'systemize the risk out' in some quite complex environments, as long as execution can be broken down into discrete actions, and variations from plan and likely contingencies are largely predictable
- Modelling and risk processes are insufficient for more reactive environments
- For those environments, it is necessary to build a culture of risk or safety in which the organizational approach and procedures are only one (necessary) part of the story:
  - Organization: regulation, supervision, training and assessment.
  - Standard operating procedures: best practice default options for common scenarios and working environments
  - Behavioural training: building awareness of the impact of one's own behaviour in terms of communication and decision-making
  - Execution: an investment of time and effort in execution excellence through planning, contingency planning, briefing and debriefing
  - Leadership: walk the talk – senior leaders must be seen to reward and recognize risk management and place it clearly at the top of their own agendas

Chapter 9

Conclusion

The only thing that stands between a man and what he wants from life
is often merely the will to try it and the faith to believe that it is possible.

Richard M DeVos

In this book, I have deconstructed my own experience of a high-performance team environment as a military pilot, together with thirteen years of learning from, and observing what does and doesn't work for, clients across a very wide range of sectors. The model I have presented is empirical, based on hard-won experience in some demanding environments. It is not a formula or a quick fix, but neither is it limited to only being applied in some perfect world in its entirety. The Figure 9.1

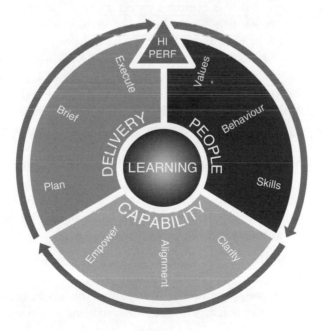

Figure 9.1 High performance model (Full)

expands on the model at Figure 1.3 and summarizes ten key factors in a sequential manner (the nine around the circle, plus learning) and there is a logic to that presentation and way of thinking. However, focusing effort on only one or some of those factors should still have a positive impact on performance. Faced with finite resources, one sensible approach is to map the team or organization's current status against the factors to give a snapshot view of areas to focus. Tools are available for that purpose; by way of an initial catalyst I have summarized each of the main groupings below, together with some key questions.

People

1. Are the organization's values consistently role-modelled?
2. Are behaviours as valued as technical or functional skills?
3. Is the aim of skill development to be best-in-class?

It is a cliché used by many organizations that their people are their greatest asset, even if it is almost invariably true. However, recruitment is often more function- than people-based. What is more important: the right person or a person who has done the same thing before, on paper at least? My own experience is that in team environments, as long as the core foundation competencies are in place, a person with a good mind and the right attitude is worth their weight in gold. Mapping the fit is difficult but possible to do scientifically, although just an informal assessment may deliver significant value. However, even that requires that the organization's values are explicit and role-modelled. You may not know the person's values but you will be able to see if their behaviour matches up with the organizational values. We saw evidence in examples as varied as Shackleton's Antarctic adventure and the Red Arrows selection of the benefit of this approach in practice.

Finally, skill development should always be done with the aim of becoming best-in-class. The individual's appetite for that is a personal issue. But it is a two-way street. The organization needs to offer the opportunity to make it happen. You will get what you train for and what you reward.

Capability

4. Does everybody have clarity in their mission and why it is important?
5. Are systems and communications processes optimized to facilitate alignment?
6. Are people trusted and empowered to act?

Since the time of the Roman Army, enlightened senior officers, and in more modern times executives, have recognized that the fog of battle or business represents an effective barrier to micromanagement and excessive control or oversight. There is also the small matter of the massively demotivating impact of such an approach. However, empowerment is not possible without clarity and alignment. We observe no bigger barrier to performance in large organizations than task and role clarity. And any time you are asking 'what', you should also be asking 'why'.

Alignment requires standard processes that can take a long time to get right, but do so and the return on the investment is disproportionately large. We saw examples of the benefits for fighter pilots and in the Red Arrows' planning process, with a salutary lesson from the Channel Tunnel project of what can happen when incentives are not aligned. Alignment also requires communication protocols to get the right information to the right people at the right time.

With clarity and alignment, it's time to set your people free. Give them some ownership and 'skin in the game' and you might be surprised at the capabilities you unleash.

Delivery

7. Is planning and plan-based execution encouraged?
8. Are briefings held to ensure common understanding?
9. Are the priorities for execution crystal clear and simple?

Delivery requires a focus on the outcome at every stage. Plans are the essential precursor but you shouldn't plan in detail for what simply can't be predicted. The aim is to deliver the outcome, not just execute the plan no matter what has changed. The value is often not in the plans, but in the planning. It is the effort and brainpower that you expend developing and stress-testing the plan that will equip the team for execution. And watch out for the hidden assumptions in your plan that you can't see due to becoming wedded to your own brilliance. Your competitors will probably not meekly follow the path you'd like them to. If Red Teams are good enough for the director of the CIA, then they may be worth considering.

Never assume that everyone's understanding of the plan is the same as yours by osmosis. Clever, highly qualified people have been doing advanced surgery around the world for hundreds of years, but the rate of adverse outcomes was dramatically reduced by the introduction of briefing processes.

No matter how well you equip your people, they will at some stage be overtaken by the noise and friction of the real world. The more complex your environment, the simpler your priorities need to be. Make sure everybody knows what the ball is that they can't afford to drop.

Learning

10. Is continuous improvement the norm?

High performance is as much as anything about learning. World-class teams have a chronic unease about their status and are constantly striving to improve. Individuals will always be looking for new ways to stretch themselves, widen the breadth of their experience and look at situations from different perspectives. Nobody ever starts anything as brilliant. The ability to maximize your rate of learning, and in competitive environments your *relative* rate of learning, is critical. Whether personal development, organizational process or learning on the job in real time through debriefing, continuous improvement must be the norm. If poor clarity is the biggest barrier to performance, debriefing is the most important tool to accelerate performance.

Other issues

We also took a quick canter through leadership (the ability to bring others on the journey with you) and risk (the ability to mitigate against adverse outcomes). The underlying theme of both was behavioural. People may be happy to work for you because you are clever or well organized, but it is leadership which will unlock their ability to reach new levels of achievement. In its truest form, leadership only exists if others choose to follow you of their own free will. That decision will be based on a multitude of visible and intangible factors but is highly likely to be predicated on your behaviour, which is the window into your values.

Risk is a specialist field and can be a minefield for the unwary. However, to be managed effectively, it needs to be understood and owned by operators. If not, it will likely become an exercise in compliance. In the final reckoning, it is another performance metric or KPI, even if for some industries it is their single most important KPI. Like any other performance factor, on complex tasks and in large complicated organizations, it can't be micromanaged; the decision-making has to be decentralized. The more you are reactive to factors outside your control, the truer this is.

And finally

To finish, I return to some of my initial themes. Excellence is a habit. The factors that drive it are simple, but consistently delivering against them is not. However, beware of confusing difficulty with complexity. It's all about world-class basics. Get them right and anything is possible.

Notes

1 The crux of the issue

1 'Unconscious competence' is the highest stage of competence in the model used by psychologists to describe skill acquisition. When operating in this mode, the task is semi-automated in the brain and it is not necessary to focus in detail on every aspect in order to successfully complete it. At this level of competence, a task will require less mental capacity or processing power than at any of the previous levels: unconscious incompetence, conscious incompetence and conscious competence. The model is attributed to Noel Birch, developed during his time at Gordon Training International.
2 Pattern recognition is intrinsically connected to the concept of unconscious competence in that when we are expert in a task, we can often recognize variations from the norm without needing to actively monitor all the details or variables. The relevance of this factor to decision-making has been the subject of much research, in particular by Gary Klein and colleagues. See for instance: G. Klein (1998), *Sources of Power: How People Make Decisions*. Cambridge, MA: MIT Press.
3 The concepts of multitasking and attention spans are very effectively examined by J. Medina (2008), *Brain Rules*. Seattle, WA: Pear Press, in particular, pp. 84–97, 90. A good example of producing simplicity from complexity is provided in the Marks & Spencer case study in this book's Chapter 5C. Sir Stuart Rose simplified the whole business down to only three priorities: product, service and environment.
4 S. Bungay (2011), *The Art of Action*. London: Nicholas Brealey Publishing.

2 Excellence – it starts with you

1 M. Gladwell (2008), *Outliers*. London: Allen Lane.
2 M. Syed (2010), *Bounce*. London: Fourth Estate.
3 J. C. Collins (2001), *Good to Great*. London: Random House.
4 Team Sky was founded as a professional cycling team in 2010 with the express aim of producing a clean (drug-free) first British winner of the Tour de France within five years. The aim was achieved when (now Sir) Bradley Wiggins became the first Briton to win in 2012, followed by Chris Froome in 2013, who repeated the feat in 2015. In a sport dominated by the use of performance-enhancing drugs, Team Sky's success has been the subject of much suspicion and accusation. However, at the time of writing, not a shred of evidence has been offered to back up those accusations.

5 C. Woodward (2004), *Winning !* London: Hodder & Stoughton. Woodward drew lessons from multiple sources including on a 'happy workplace' from a dentist he met in Australia, Dr Paddi Lund, who became Australia's most successful dentist by only treating the 5 per cent of his patients whose company he actually enjoyed (and asking for referrals to their friends). See also: P. Lund (1995), *Building the Happiness-Centred Business*. Bulimba: Solutions Press Business Publishing Ltd.
6 S. Wetlaufer (2001), 'The perfect paradox of star brands: an interview with Bernard Arnault of LVMH', *Harvard Business Review*, 10.

3 Team players for team games (People)

1 J. R. Katzenbach and D. K. Smith (1993), *The Wisdom of Teams*. Maidenhead: McGraw-Hill.
2 S. Kerr (1975), 'On the folly of rewarding A, while hoping for B', *Academy of Management Journal*, Volume 18, Number 4, 769–783.
3 J. Welch and S. Welch (2005), *Winning*. London: HarperCollins.
4 L. A. Cunningham (2009), *The Essays of Warren Buffet: Lessons for Investors and Managers*. Singapore: John Wiley and Sons (third edition).
5 A. Kohn (1993), 'Why incentive plans cannot work', *Harvard Business Review*, 9.

4 Building the teams and organization you need (Capability)

1 W. Isaacson (2011), *Steve Jobs*. London: Little Brown.
2 The Channel Tunnel has been the subject of extensive academic and general press coverage, most often in the context of what went wrong. The following case study, edited by Anbari F. T., 'The Chunnel Project', The George Washington University, is freely available online and gives a good overview of the main issues and was the primary reference source for the material presented here: http://www.pmi.org/~/media/PDF/Academic/case%20studies/Chunnel%20Project.ashx
3 In both the Channel Tunnel project and the construction of Wembley Stadium (another project that became a case study for the wrong reasons), the outstanding engineering was heavily overshadowed by cost overruns. A large contributory factor in both cases was the award of the contract to the lowest bidder despite the number of technology unknowns to be addressed. The lessons appear to have been learnt for major programmes, but similar thinking is still being applied in smaller projects. We recently observed a property development company invest significant effort in the alignment of stakeholders, but still commit the main contractor to a fixed-price deal, thereby providing instant misalignment of interests (the developer wants quality but the contractor is heavily incentivized to protect the margins). A similar theme can be seen in some of the history of rail franchise awards by the UK government. See for example, the following newspaper article: A. Trotman and N. Thomas (2012), 'Richard

Branson attacks Government "insanity" after Virgin Trains loses West Coast rail contract', *The Daily Telegraph*, 15 August 12. The article is viewable online at: http://www.telegraph.co.uk/finance/newsbysector/transport/9476519/Richard-Branson-attacks-Government-insanity-after-Virgin-Trains-loses-West-Coast-rail-contract.html

4 As a result of learning from major project failings caused by intrinsic misalignment between stakeholders, a partnership relationship was adopted in the construction of London Heathrow T5. The following case study provides a useful overview of the programme: J. Harrison and M. Bartlett, 'Case study 2 – Heathrow Terminal 5 – a new paradigm for major programme risk management', *The Institute of Risk Management*. It is viewable online at: https://www.theirm.org/media/1055871/case_study2.pdf

5A Plans and planning

1 S. McChrystal, C. Collins, C. Fussell, and D. Silverman (2015), *Team of Teams*. New York: Portfolio/Penguin.
2 The search for purpose is the raison d'être of most religions and appears to be a basic human need. A sense of purpose in the professional environment can be a significant source of motivation and engagement. In his highly regarded book on the subject, Daniel Pink identifies three key sources of engagement: autonomy, mastery and purpose. See D. Pink (2009), *Drive*. New York: Riverhead Books.
3 Bruce Tuckman identified four key stages that most teams follow on the path to high performance: forming (polite getting to know each other), storming (internal challenge and pushing the boundaries formed), norming (resolution of differences and development of commitments) and performing (self-explanatory). The model has stood the test of time over fifty years: B. Tuckman (1965), 'Developmental Sequence in Small Groups', *Psychological Bulletin*, 63 (6), 384–399.
4 E. M. Rasiel and P. N. Friga (2001), *The McKinsey Mind*. New York: McGraw-Hill
5 An example of IDEO's process was captured on ABC's Nightline programme, versions of which can be viewed online at a number of locations.
6 A good insight into the sequence of high-level decision-making can be seen in the History Network's documentary, *Targeting Bin Laden*, first shown in the United States on 6 September 2011. The programme includes highly credible interviewees including President Obama, National Security Adviser Tom Donilon, White House counterterrorism adviser John Brennan and former CIA officials.

5B Communicating the plan

1 The Charge of the Light Brigade is well documented. The references used here were John Chapman's analysis for Cranfield University's School of Management Praxis Centre (viewable here: http://www.som.cranfield.ac.uk/som/p4753/knowledge/praxis-centre/articles/praxis-articles) and N. F. Dixon (1979), *On the Psychology of Military of Military Incompetence*. London: Futura Publications.

2 A. B. Haynes, T. G. Weiser, W. R. Berry, S. R. Lipsitz, A.-H. S. Breizat, E. P. Dellinger, T. Herbosa, S. Joseph, P. L. Kibatala, M. C. M. Lapitan, A. F. Merry, K. Moorthy, R. K. Reznick, B. Taylor and A. A. Gawande (2009), 'A surgical safety checklist to reduce morbidity and mortality in a global population', *New England Journal of Medicine*, 360, 491–499.
3 I. A. Walker, S. Reshamwalla and I. H. Wilson (2012), 'Surgical safety checklists: do they improve outcomes?', *British Journal of Anaesthesia*, 109 (1), 47–54.

5C Execution

1 M. Gladwell (2005), *Blink*. London: Penguin.
2 The idea of automatic or semi-automatic comparison of a situation with a mental model is a key factor in a wide range of decision-making and performance under pressure scenarios. In addition to Gladwell's hypothesis and Klein's work (Chapter 1, note 2), academics from diverse fields have converged on a similar concept of two types of decision making, which might be described as automatic and manual. Two seminal thinkers who have influenced my own thoughts considerably are Prof Daniel Kahneman and Dr Steve Peters. S. Kahneman (2011), *Thinking, Fast and Slow*. London: Penguin. S. Peters (2012), *The Chimp Paradox*. London: Vermillion.
3 S. Rose (2007), 'Back in Fashion', *Harvard Business Review*, 4; M&S Press release: 'Marks and Spencer Group plc Summary Operational Review', 12 July 2004; and personal interview Author/Stuart Rose, April 2009.
4 There is a nice analogy here with McChrystal's approach in a rather different hostile and reactive environment in Iraq (note 1, Chapter 5A). During his tenure, McChrystal placed an ever increasing emphasis on information sharing which eventually resulted in a global daily video conference call, personally chaired by him, which all key players took part in.

6 Accelerating performance (Learning)

1 Data source: NHS England website: http://www.nhs.uk/NHSEngland/thenhs/about/Pages/overview.aspx
2 'An Organisation with a Memory' was published by the UK Department of Health on 13 June 2000. It can be downloaded from a number of healthcare and NHS sites including: https://www.aagbi.org/sites/default/files/An%20organisation%20with%20a%20memory.pdf
3 Haddon-Cave C. (2009), *The Nimrod Review*. Viewable online at: https://www.gov.uk/government/uploads/system/uploads/attachment_data/file/229037/1025.pdf
4 Chief Counsel's Report (2011), 'Macondo: The Gulf oil disaster', National Commission on the BP Deepwater Horizon Oil Spill and Offshore Drilling, see for example, https://bookstore.gpo.gov/products/sku/999-000-55552-1.
5 J. L. Thorogood (2015), 'The Macondo inflow test decision: implications for well

control and non-technical skills training', prepared for presentation at the SPE/IADC Drilling Conference and Exhibition held in London, UK, 17–19 March 2015.

6 There is no one definitive source of the origin and development of after action review, however the following contains an interesting overview of military and commercial application: M. Darling, C. Parry and J. Moore (2005), 'Learning in the thick of it', *Harvard Business Review*, 6.

7 On 8 May 2009, *The Daily Telegraph* 'broke' the story of the MPs' expenses scandal. The story had actually been generating momentum for some time ever since questions were asked on the subject by journalists in 2005 on the implementation of the Freedom of Information Act 2000. However enquiries had met with legal challenge and stonewalling at every stage. It wasn't until a whistleblower leaked details to the newspaper on the House of Commons' authorities' documentation of MPs' second home claims that the floodwaters finally broke. The scandal proved to be a seminal moment for parliament with a disproportionate number of MPs not seeking re-election at the next election in 2010.

8 There has only been one female Red Arrows pilot to date largely due to simple numbers of those available and applying. Female pilots are still a small minority in the RAF and to be selected a pilot would have to have been selected for fast-jet flying, stayed in long enough to gain sufficient experience, demonstrated the requisite ability and actually applied for the job. Given the small percentage of women starting training in the first place, very few will emerge from the above pipeline at the right time with right experience, apply and get selected. On a positive note though, the process is a genuine meritocracy and those who do get selected are there for no other reason than that they earned it.

7 Bringing others on the journey (Leadership)

1 Many libraries of books have been written about Churchill. For an overview of his relationship with his individual generals, see: J. Keegan (ed.) (1991), *Churchill's Generals*. London: Cassell.

2 IQ is a measure of cognitive ability and intelligence and has been assessed under that name since the start of the twentieth century. EQ only emerged at the end of that century, largely popularized by Goleman's book (next note). It is a measure of self-awareness of one's own and others' emotional state.

3 D. Goleman (1995), *Emotional Intelligence: Why It Can Matter More Than IQ*. New York: Bantam Books.

4 In this context, Enigma actually referred to the cypher machines used by the German military in the Second World War. Initial variants were cracked by Polish codebreakers but the pivotal breakthrough in that conflict came from the British team at Bletchley Park. The most striking example of the issue referred to in the text remains unconfirmed and contentious to this day. It concerns reports that Churchill was aware of a massive raid (Operational Moonlight Sonata) to be launched against Coventry but

failed to release the information in order to avoid letting the Germans know that the code had been cracked.

5 The 1994 crash of a USAF B52 aircraft at Fairchild Air Force Base has been the subject of extensive analysis, review and case study, the last most often in the context of leadership and human factors issues. The scenario I described here was one small but significant item within a wider context and sequence of events. The base commander was of the opinion that the display pilot for the B52 had broken the rules during an airshow practice but his head of operations, who was on the aircraft, assured him that was not the case. The base commander did not pursue the issue further and on the next practice, the pilot crashed the aircraft, killing himself and three other crew members.

6 Boyd's story offers some fascinating insights into leadership, objectivity, evidence-based decision making, organizational dynamics and the pursuit of excellence. It is well told in Robert Coram's biography: R. Coram (2002), *Boyd: The Fighter Pilot Who Changed the Art of War*. New York: Little, Brown and Company.

8 Missing sink holes (Risk)

1 R. Clay-Williams (2013), 'Military rather than civil aviation holds the answers for safer healthcare', *BMJ*, 347.

2 W. Rankin (2007), 'MEDA investigation process', *AERO*, Quarter 2, 2007, 3. *AERO* magazine is published quarterly by Boeing Commercial Airplanes and is distributed at no cost to operators of Boeing commercial airplanes. It is available online and the relevant article can be viewed here: http://www.boeing.com/commercial/aeromagazine/articles/qtr_2_07/AERO_Q207_article3.pdf

3 There is extensive literature relating to CRM concepts and no one definitive source as to the key factors however there is broad agreement among most experts in principle, and very little variation of the key factors across different working environments. Aviation has tended to lead the way, having picked up the mantle from NASA. The reason for the aviation's lead is most likely simply a function of consequences. Aviation accidents often involve many fatalities and tend to be high-profile. Other industries where the consequences of error are also high have followed over time, for example, energy and healthcare in particular.

4 R. L. Helmreich and A. C. Merritt (1998), *Culture at Work in Aviation and Medicine*. Aldershot: Ashgate Publishing.

5 C. Duhigg (2013), *The Power of Habit*. London: Random House

6 E. A. Cohen (2002), *Supreme Command*. New York: Simon & Schuster

7 F. Maclean (2009), *Eastern Approaches*. London: Penguin.

8 The seeds of this analogy were sown in my mind by Pablo Triana's book: P. Triana (2008), *Lecturing Birds on Flying*. Hoboken, NJ: John Wiley & Sons.

9 This line of thinking, and many related themes dealing with probability, forecasting and randomness have been developed extensively by Nassim Nicholas Taleb. His best known work is: N. N. Taleb (2007), *The Black Swan: The Impact of the Highly Improbable*. New York: Penguin.

Index